LOST iN Europe

The inspiration for our book arose from frequent inquiries by our friends asking for our favourite lunch spot in London or a shopping destination in Naples. Each time, we crafted a guide, leading to requests for our personal top 10 in various cities. Our concept was to compile our personal favourites from different cities into a single booklet.

We themed this book, which includes 25 European cities, around the senses: SEE for architecture and public spaces, TASTE for restaurants, TOUCH for shopping and markets, and SMELL for nightlife.

In terms of content selection, this LOST iN book again stands out by focusing on the identity and personality of each venue, avoiding generic recommendations. When exploring cities like Zurich, we discovered a public swimming pool from 1909 located in a river. In Stockholm, we found a brutalist restaurant serving only one ingredient per dish. In Antwerp, we unearthed the best vintage store for independent creators and enjoyed dancing to Afrobeat sounds in a micro club in Madrid.

To enhance the experience, we included a movie and a city-specific playlist. We avoided generic views here too, focusing instead on unique aspects of the musical scene in each city. For instance, we explored Antwerp's surprising ambient scene and Barcelona's diverse Rumba Catalana. The photography, while not depicting the people from the city, shows an intimate and personal perspective of the city.

LOST iN Europe delves into what unifies European cities despite their diversity. Europe shares a common history and cultural backbone, yet their unique characteristics stand out. From architecture to social dynamics, Europe's cities exhibit distinct traits while maintaining a sense of cohesion due to their proximity and cultural exchange.

You might not always immediately notice what unifies all these cities, but it's often perceptible in the spaces between locations. Although it is hard to discern a common thread, a subtle but distinctive European characteristic is the tendency of people to congregate outside locations, not just inside. This trait, contrasting with other cultural tendencies, is evident from Edinburgh to Marseille. Additionally, Europe's unique position, where many countries coexist in close proximity, leads to extreme diversity while maintaining nearness. This fosters cultural exchange and distinctively amplifies local particularities.

The format and design were inspired by 1970s maps found in the glove box of your grandparents' Alfa, resembling a beaten-up Michelin guide printed on thin paper with monochromatic photos. These guides were both collectible and designed to age well. In collaboration with Studio NODE, we aimed to capture the right optical experience and design.

Our hope is that readers will be inspired to support independent, characterful local businesses, celebrating personality rather than user-generated ratings. Our selections range from new, innovative concepts to century-old establishments, emphasizing unique approaches and authenticity. In essence, the book is about celebrating the unique character of each location, providing a rich, multi-dimensional view of Europe.

AMSTERDAM

“Some tourists think Amsterdam is a city of sin, but in truth it is a city of freedom. And in freedom, most people find sin.”

John Green

S E E

Vondelpark

The perfect location for a walk or, better yet, a bike ride. Even in the colder months of the year, a true Amsterdammer maintains that strong bond with their bicycle. Artist Amy Dicke suggests a winter ride at nightfall, to watch all of the bike lights moving through the park.

→1071

NDSM

After the shipyard's closure in 1984, squatters took over the abandoned docks, followed by artists, creatives and entrepreneurs. First Café Noorderlicht opened, drawing an alternative crowd, and the Wharf became an established venue for festivals. Now an art city and indoor market occupy the spacious halls, and you'll find chic restaurants like Bistro Noord and trendy bars like Pllek.

→NDSM-Plein 28, 1033 WB

Hortus Botanicus

This is one of the oldest botanical gardens in the world and it's best enjoyed on warm summer nights. There's something magical that you can only experience at a late hour: wonderful sounds of whistling that may remind you of birds—but actually, it's frogs.

→Plantage Middenlaan 2a, 1018 DD
→020 625 9021

Stedelijk Museum

The largest Dutch museum of contemporary art and design, Stedelijk has been around since 1895 and received a new modern wing, known as the 'bathtub,' in 2012 by Benthem Crouwel Architects. With more than 90,000 artworks and objects from 1870 to the present, you'll find works from prime names such as Cézanne, Chagall, Koons, Warhol, and Picasso but also movements such as Bauhaus and De Stijl.

→Museumplein 10, 1071 DJ
→020 573 2911

Pythonbrug

Connecting Sporenburg and Borneo Island, the red Pythonbrug, with its undulating form, exemplifies Dutch innovative design. This pedestrian bridge offers an exceptional vantage point over the Eastern Docklands area, ideal for a peaceful, reflective stroll.

→Pythonbrug, 1019 AX

T A S T E

Haring en Zo

Sample traditional Dutch herring at this local favourite, prepared in the time-honoured way: raw and served with onions and pickles.

→Nieuwezijds Voorburgwal 200, 1012 RR
→06 51952882

de Willem

De Willem holds the key to a hidden Amsterdam, away from the typical city bustle. Amidst the historical charm of its canal-side location, this quaint bar invites you to indulge in a thoughtfully curated collection of craft beers and spirits. Its rustic and authentic setting offers a glimpse of traditional Dutch culture, mirrored in its well-honed hospitality.

→Haarlemmerplein 66, 1013 HS

AMSTERDAM

Rijsel

Tucked away off a residential street, the concept behind this elegant restaurant is based on a passion for French cooking. The result is a no-nonsense menu, affordable and cooked to perfection (a three-course menu costs just under 35 euros). Be sure to reserve your table in advance.

→Marcusstraat 52, 1091 TK
→020 463 2142

Euro Pizza Restaurant

Offering hand-tossed pizzas and vibrant Italian flavours, Euro Pizza Restaurant is an unassuming gem located in Amsterdam's multicultural Southeast district. Enjoy the inviting ambience and fresh ingredients that together serve to capture the essence of traditional Italian pizza making.

→Gedempt Hamerkanaal 79, 1021 KP
→020 895 0843

Bak Restaurant

Up on the third floor of the warehouse-turned-theatre Het Veem, overlooking the IJ river, is Bak. Originally a pop-up operating in empty spaces across the city, it laid roots here. Its changing menu of ethically sourced dishes includes well-thought-out combinations like roe deer stew and bone marrow terrine with charred kale, or celeriac with pine ice cream for dessert.

→Van Diemenstraat 408, 1013 CR 0
→20 737 2553

De Kas

A greenhouse that once belonged to Amsterdam's municipal nursery is now partly a restaurant. Most of the vegetables, fruits and herbs are grown in-house, so everything is in season, harvested in the morning, and served that same day.

→Kamerlingh Onneslaan 3, 1097 DE
→020 462 4562

Cornerstore

Cornerstore offers a curated selection of design items and homeware, representing Amsterdam's modern aesthetic. The boutique showcases a mix of local and international brands, each carefully chosen for their craft and design quality.

→Papaverweg 11, 1032 KD
→020 239 0062

Wilde Zwijnen

The restaurant Wilde Zwijnen was a trendsetter for the “New Dutch Cuisine”, spawning many imitators, but few can match its pared-down tasting menus from locally sourced produce. Make sure to book in advance or, if tables are scarce, head to the rustic eatery’s ‘younger brother,’ Eetbar next door serving tapas-style small plates inspired by the French and Spanish kitchens.

→Javaplein 23, 1095 CJ Amsterdam, Netherlands
→020 463 3043

Cafe Modern

The people from Hotel De Goudfazant were determined to feed more mouths in Amsterdam, and so opened a second eatery in the shape of Café Modern. Located in a former bank, pared-back furniture meets with the old-world style of this once commercial building. Even the bathrooms pay tribute, set into the bank’s former safe. As with many good Amsterdam restaurants, Café Modern offers a table d’hôte of four courses with seasonal ingredients.

→Meidoornweg 2, 1031 GG
→020 494 0684

Breda

Upscale but relaxed, a refined kitchen but without the giant price tag—this restaurant ticks all the right boxes when it comes to finding a great place for lunch or dinner. Go for the blind four, six or eight course menu, which could feature anything from sous vide cod to airy artichoke soup.

→Singel 210, 1016 AB
→020 622 5233

T O U C H

Noordermarkt

Saturday mornings are best spent at this lively flea market. All sorts of vintage treasures await, while farmers from all around Amsterdam bring in the freshest food for you to feast on. Wander into the Boerenmarkt section to shop the best selection of meat, herbs and cheeses.

→Noordermarkt, 1015 NA Amsterdam, Netherlands

Droog

Stylish, somewhat affordable, and an institution, Droog is a rabbit hole of discoveries. There’s accommodation in the One and Only Bedroom situated in the roof, events at the space Hôtel Droog, high tea and good coffee at the Droog Café and the Fairy Tale Garden offering a glimpse into gardening done the Droog way. An essential of Dutch design, this spot has been supplying the world with collaborations, concepts and anti-disciplinary design.

→Staalstraat 7B, 1011 JJ
→020 523 5050

Concrete Matters

Designers used to float into Amsterdam in pursuit of inspiration, but the flood has dried up as vintage stores dwindled in number and quality. For the real thing without markup or up-cycling of chain thrift shop wares, head to Concrete Matters, an old-world secondhand store whose owner has a keen eye for a silhouette and designer clothing with a story as well as a selection of rare Americana.

→Gasthuismolensteeg 12, 1016 AN
→020 261 0933

Hermès Store

The Hermès Store in Amsterdam, housed in a majestic canal house, is an opulent showcase of this luxury brand's craftsmanship. The meticulously restored 17th-century interior and artfully displayed collection are a testament to the brand's commitment to artistry and heritage.

→Pieter Cornelisz Hooftstraat 94, 1071 CC
→020 305 7050

Athenaeum Boekhandel

An iconic Amsterdam bookstore, you'll find all manner of printed matter at Athenaeum. From Dutch and international newspapers to an exhaustive selection of independent magazines, this bookshop has a loyal following that loves to spend an afternoon browsing the titles. Of course, the independent shop also has a solid selection of fiction and non-fiction books in Dutch as well as English.

→Spui 14-16, 1012 XA
→020 514 1460

S M E L L

Shelter

One of Amsterdam's havens for quality dance music, Shelter was created with design and sound quality very much in the foreground. House and Techno are at the heart of this club where the vanguards of electronica make the crowds travel to other dimensions (musically speaking).

→Overhoeksplein 3, 1031 KS

AMSTERDAM

Garage Noord

Welcome to "a club for everyone", but especially those who crave an eclectic, late-night atmosphere. This establishment is a hybrid, combining a gallery space and restaurant, but it truly shines as an intimate club, offering an authentic blend of a dive bar and disco vibe. The musical menu varies depending on the host – but DJs usually know how to fill a floor.

→Gedempt Hamerkanaal 40, 1021 KM
→06 23320638

Red Light Records

The record store shop is not only a treasure trove for vinyl collectors with a carefully curated selection of rare and eclectic records. Located in the same tiny complex as the record shop Vintage Voudou and Red Light Radio, catching up on the latest news about Amsterdam's underground nightlife is mandatory.

→Oudezijds Achterburgwal 133, 1012 DG
→06 17002017

Door 74

For exquisite cocktails, head to the pioneer of speakeasy bars in the Netherlands. It comes in the shape of an old-school gentlemen's club, with tin ceiling, antique barware and so on. The entrance is behind an inconspicuous black façade. Make sure to reserve a table, it usually gets crowded.

→Reguliersdwarsstraat 74, 1017 BN
→06 82042977

De School

The multidisciplinary space housed in a former technical school offers a blend of wonderful club nights – especially during the summer with access to an open-air space – plus a restaurant and a gallery. Watch also out for special label showcases, concerts and performances.

→Doctor Jan van Breemenstraat 3, 1056 AB
→020 737 3197

H E A R

F I L M

Amsterdamned, Dick Maas, 1988

Set against the backdrop of Amsterdam's scenic canals, this suspenseful crime thriller follows the city's hardened detective as he attempts to solve a series of gruesome murders. Plunged into the heart of Amsterdam's darker side, he's caught in a high-stakes game of cat and mouse with a maniacal killer.

ANTWERP

"Antwerp is like eating an entire box of chocolates."

Anonymous

S E E

Béguinage

A haven of tranquillity amidst the city. In the garden, fruit trees are planted and a pond is created. The origin of the establishment dates back to the 13th century. Until the 1980s, female members of the Beguines, a Christian community dedicated to charitable purposes, still lived here.

→Rodestraat 39, 2000

Middelheim Park

Middelheim Park intertwines nature and art, presenting an open-air museum set against the canvas of lush greenery. It houses a collection of over 200 sculptures, providing a. perspective to the global art scene. The park is a harmonious blend of creativity and tranquillity.

→Middelheimlaan 1, 2020
→03 288 33 60

MAS

The Museum aan de Stroom (MAS) encapsulates the city's rich past and vibrant present. Housed in a stunningly modern architectural marvel, designed by Neutelings Riedijk Architects from Rotterdam, it presents a multitude of perspectives on the city, from its history as a port city to its dynamic contemporary culture.

→Hanzestedenplaats 1, 2000
→03 338 44 00

ModeMuseum

ModeMuseum (MoMu), Antwerp's fashion museum, weaves a narrative of the city's influential role in the global fashion scene. Its rotating exhibits capture the city's sartorial spirit, from historical textiles to contemporary couture, reflecting the creativity of Antwerp's famed fashion designers like Martin Margiela, Dirk Bikkembergs or Dries Van Noten.

→Nationalestraat 28, 2000
→03 470 27 70

Havenhuis

The Port House, or Havenhuis, is a striking fusion of past and future, symbolizing Antwerp's status as a global port. Designed by Zaha Hadid, the spaceship-like structure dramatically surmounts the original fire station building, offering a visual dialogue between the city's architectural heritage and forward-thinking design.

→Havenhuis, Entrepotkaai 1, 2000

S M E L L

Café Hopper

The laid-back café and a jazz bar offer an inviting terrace during the days and live music during the night. An Antwerp nightlife classic for grown-ups.

→Leopold de Waelstraat 2, 2000

Ampère

The flagship of the Antwerp techno scene. International DJs like Laurent Garnier or Sven Vaeth are feeding the brilliant sound system. Their own digital wallet (app) is needed for ordering drinks. Nice: the destination is committed to sustainable clubbing.

→Simonsstraat 21, 2018
→03 232 09 23

Marigold

A cozy cocktail bar with a nostalgic and Art Deco charm. The architects at Studio Stranger have curated the vintage ambiance, adorning the space with softly glowing lights, gleaming polished wood, and cascading drapes. Music is played on vinyl. Ask for their signature cocktails.

→Vrijdagmarkt 18, 2000

TheCommon

Another classic techno venue. The place got a major make-over in 2022. The crowd dances till the morning under neon light on two floors.

→Straatsburgdok Noordkaai 3, 2030

Club Vaag

Small basement club with an underground vibe. Sometimes it can get narrow and too busy. Drinks are not a bargain.

→Rijnkaai 4, 2000

T A S T E

Ciro's

With a mastery of traditional recipes and a focus on fresh, local ingredients, Ciro's offers an intimate glimpse into the city's gastronomic heritage. Delighting both residents and visitors, this traditional brasserie showcases classic Belgian cuisine at its finest. Try the classics like Steak Ciro with six sauces or veal sweetbread with spinach.

→Amerikalei 6, 2000
→03 238 11 47

Elfde Gebod

Step back in time at Elfde Gebod, a charmingly antiquated cafe that doubles as an exhibition space for religious art and icons. Its quirky yet nostalgic atmosphere offers a refreshing break from the urban hustle.

→Torfbrug 10, 2000
→03 288 57 33

Le John

Hidden behind the facade of the art deco Sint-Lievenscollege, this bar restaurant features natural wines and refined dishes with an Italian touch. The retro-chic decor makes it a cute destination for intimate dinners.

→Kasteelpleinstraat 25, 2000
→0488 09 09 12

Graanmarkt 13

This concept is aesthetically and architecturally satisfying and offers a unique selection of timeless objects, a vegetable-focused restaurant with accolades, and a luxurious apartment for short and long stays.

→Graanmarkt 13, 2000
→03 337 79 92

Native

A biocuisine restaurant that lays emphasis on organic ingredients. The menu offers an exploration of the region's gastronomic potential, and their zero-waste philosophy adds an extra layer of responsibility to the experience.

→Muntstraat 8, 2000
→0478 40 07 11

Veranda

The modern restaurant with an industrial but warm ambiance offers exceptional culinary experiences. Try the affordable tasting menus, centered around seasonal products and natural wines.

→Lange Lobroekstraat 34, 2060
→03 218 55 95

Album

Chef Joris Gielen and host Toon Craen oversee a hybrid establishment offering coffee, breakfast, lunch, and their renowned homemade sourdough bread. Their menu features diverse dishes like beef tartare with makreel vinaigrette and beetroot, gravlax, and a spiegelei with roasted lettuce, kimchi, and bacon, focusing on light, flavourful options for an energetic start to the day or a revitalizing break.

→Vlaamsekaai 6, 2000
→03 334 88 59

Le Pristine

Le Pristine brings a distinctive twist to the dining scene in Antwerp by infusing Italian flair into local ingredients. Its culinary philosophy is rooted in seasonality and authenticity, resulting in a menu that perfectly complements its stylish and art-centric setting.

→Lange Gasthuisstraat 13, 2000
→03 376 33 76

Tazu

A contemporary cornerstone in Antwerp's culinary landscape, Tazu effortlessly marries Japanese aesthetics with European gastronomic techniques, delivering an exceptional fusion of flavours that cater to discerning taste buds.

→Vlaaikensgang 8a, 2000
→03 246 46 09

Have a Roll

With its vibrant yet unpretentious setting, Have a Roll puts a unique spin on traditional sushi rolls, infusing them with a Belgian touch. From seafood to vegetarian, each roll is crafted with locally sourced ingredients.

→Oudaan 15/31, 2000

T O U C H

Dries Van Noten

The boutique of one of the city's iconic fashion designers does not require a purchase, window shopping is recommended as well. Because of its location right in the middle of the fashion district and next to the fashion museum, this stylish spot mirrors the eclectic essence of Van Noten's collections and adds a visual layer to the city's chic aesthetic.

→Nationalestraat 16, 2000
→03 470 25 10

DelRey

DelRey is a key destination for chocolate lovers, representing the rich tradition of Belgian chocolaterie. Their array of exquisite pralines and pastries invites visitors to indulge in a gastronomic experience.

→Appelmansstraat 5, 2018
→03 470 28 61

La fille d'O

The lingerie is a bit like their campaigns: slightly contradictory, and changing what society considers a role model today. The models (skinny, full-figured, pale, tanned, tattooed, pimpled, scarred) are the living proof.

→Kasteelpleinstraat 64, 2000
→03 257 24 94

Ann Demeulemeester

The Ann Demeulemeester flagship store opened in 2021. It reflects the designer's poetic balance between strength and sensitivity. The location is a serene space in black and white mirroring Antwerp's avant-garde fashion sensibility.

→Leopold de Waelplaats, 2000
→03 216 01 33

Coccodrillo

The shop offers curated pre-loved fashion from a lot of Belgian designers. The selection also includes one-off pieces and runway samples. The monthly window installations showcase emerging talents from Antwerp's Royal Academy of Fine Arts, providing exposure to younger designers.

→Arenbergstraat 2, 2000
→03 233 20 93

H E A R

F I L M

Any Way the Wind Blows, Tom Barman, 2003

Directed by Tom Barman, frontman of the Belgian rock band dEUS. Set in the bustling city of Antwerp, the film revolves around the final show of the fictional music legend Frank Pop, and his band The Lipstick Traces. As Frank announces his departure from the music scene, fans, band members, and opportunists congregate around the venue, each with their unique expectations and motives.

ATHENS

"How great are the dangers I face to win a good name in Athens."

Alexander The Great

S E E

Angelos & Leto Katakouzenos Foundation

Housed in a historic 19th-century mansion, the Angelos & Leto Katakouzenos Foundation is a captivating celebration of Greek culture, hosting a myriad of exhibitions and performances across disciplines.

→Leof. Vasilisis Amalias 4, 105 57
→21 0322 2144

Benaki Museum

Home to a vast collection of Greek art, the Benaki Museum showcases the cultural history of Greece from antiquity to modern times. Art enthusiasts will appreciate the variety of mediums, including ceramics, sculpture, painting, and textiles, that tell the story of the country's rich artistic heritage.

→Koumpari 1, 106 74
→21 0367 1000

Odeon of Herodes Atticus

The Odeon of Herodes Atticus, an ancient theatre nestled on the southern slopes of the Acropolis, invites a journey back in time. Regularly hosting performances, its captivating acoustics and timeless charm offer a spectacle that marries the magic of art with history.

→Dionysiou Areopagitou, 105 55
→21 0324 1807

Polis Hammam

Inspired by the tradition of the Ottoman baths, Polis Hammam provides a soothing respite from the city's hustle. The spa offers a blend of relaxation and wellness rituals, promising a peaceful retreat that stands as a testament to Athens' multicultural past.

→Avliton 6-8, 105 54
→21 0321 2020

Cinema VOX

Cinema VOX, a quaint open-air cinema, serves as a charming setting for movie aficionados to enjoy Greek and international films. Its retro charm and relaxed atmosphere make for an entertaining summer night under the stars, offering a unique twist to a classic pastime.

→Themistokleous 82, 106 81
→21 0381 0727

S M E L L

EKEI

EKEI serves as a culinary canvas where innovative Greek cuisine intertwines with contemporary international influences. This gastronomic adventure is complemented by a sophisticated ambiance and impeccable service.

→Lekka 23, 105 62
→697 192 0754

Perivoli Touranou

Tucked away in the heart of Athens, Perivoli Touranou offers a leafy retreat where one can enjoy traditional Greek music along with local delicacies in a relaxed and inviting atmosphere.

→Lisikratous 19, 105 58
→21 0323 5517

Bsideathens

Bsideathens, an atmospheric wine bar, offers a well-curated selection of Greek wines, providing a platform for local winemakers to share their craft with a wider audience.

→Mavrokordatou 6, 106 78
→21 1216 6333

Crust Basement

Crust Basement's selection of craft beers and artisanal pizzas, combined with its raw, urban aesthetic, positions it as a relaxed yet energetic meeting point within Athens' gastronomic scene.

→Protogenous 13, 105 54
→21 0325 7179

Barro Negro

Barro Negro stands as an ode to the traditions of Mexican cuisine. The restaurant's tastefully vibrant setting, combined with the innovative twists on classic dishes, makes for a spirited dining experience.

→Ioannou Paparrigopoulou 15, 105 61
→21 0010 7618

Holy Church of the Virgin Mary Gorgoepikoos and Saint Eleutherius

One of the oldest Byzantine churches in Athens, reveals a different side to the city's historical canvas. Its picturesque structure offers a glimpse into Athens' rich past, making it a haven for those interested in architectural heritage.

→Plateía Mitropóleos 8, 105 56
→21 0322 1308

T A S T E

Soil Restaurant

At Soil Restaurant, sustainable dining takes center stage with an array of plant-based dishes crafted from locally sourced produce. Its charming ambiance complements the gastronomical journey into Athenian culinary arts.

→Ferekidou 5, 116 35
→21 0751 3505

Seychelles

Seychelles, a bustling tavern in the Metaxourgeio district, offers a memorable dining experience rooted in Greek culinary tradition. The evolving menu, created from locally sourced ingredients, and the vibrant atmosphere capture the essence of modern Athenian gastronomy.

→Keramikou 49, 104 36
→21 1183 4789

Cafe Avissinia

Cafe Avissinia sits in the heart of the Monastiraki flea market, offering an array of unique dishes with a view over the buzzing marketplace. Its rustic decor and traditional Greek music create an immersive cultural experience that complements the culinary delights.

→Kinetou 7, 105 55
→21 0321 7047

Savas from Monastiraki

Savas, located in Monastiraki, serves up some of the city's best souvlaki, a popular Greek fast food. With a heritage stretching back to 1922, this eatery represents a slice of Athenian history and a simple yet satisfying culinary tradition.

→Mitropoleos 86, 105 55
→21 0324 5048

Souvlaki Kostas

An institution in Athens, known for its eponymous dish. By adhering to a traditional recipe that dates back decades, it offers a taste of Greece's enduring street food culture in the lively Petralona district.

→Pl. Agias Irinis 2, 105 60
→21 0323 2971

Barbounaki Glyfada

Barbounaki Glyfada brings fresh, coastal cuisine to the southern suburbs of Athens. Serving a range of seafood dishes in a modern yet laid-back environment, this spot offers an enticing taste of the Mediterranean seaside.

→Leof. Dimarchou Aggelou Metaxa 48, Glifada 166 74
→21 0968 0651

Zaxos Grill

Zaxos Grill is a cornerstone of traditional Greek cuisine in Athens, renowned for its quality meats and casual dining atmosphere. With its commitment to locally sourced ingredients, it offers an authentic taste of the Greek culinary landscape.

→Ermou 1, Vouliagmeni 166 71
→21 0896 0352

Philos

Philos offers a blend of art, design, fashion, and food within its multifaceted space, presenting an ever-evolving sensory experience for the city's creative minds and curious explorers.

→Solonos 32, 106 73
→21 0361 9163

Wild Souls

Wild Souls, with its combination of bohemian clothing and artisanal goods, embodies the youthful and spirited vibe of Athens. It is a space that celebrates the fusion of tradition with contemporary design.

→Voulis 36, 105 57
→21 0323 1438

T O U C H

Savapile

Located in Exarchia, Savapile is a well-loved bookshop that also serves as a cultural hub for locals. The eclectic selection of books, coupled with its commitment to promoting local authors, offers a literary exploration that parallels the spirit of this bohemian neighbourhood.

→Agias Eleousis 14, 105 54
→21 0321 7087

Olgianna Melissinos

An artisanal sandal shop, carries forward a tradition dating back to the 1920s. Famous for its handcrafted leather sandals, the shop draws visitors keen to own a piece of timeless Greek craftsmanship.

→Normanou 7, 105 55
→21 0331 1925

Monastiraki Flea Market

A bustling maze of streets filled with antique, artisan, and novelty shops, offers an engaging shopping experience. It is an embodiment of Athens' vibrant spirit, where treasures can be found at every corner.

→Ifestou 2, 105 55
→694 608 6114

Forget Me Not

A boutique gift shop in Plaka, offers an array of locally made, design-led souvenirs. With its curated selection of Greek brands, it offers a modern, stylish interpretation of the traditional souvenir shop.

→Adrianoy 100, 105 58
→21 0325 3740

Val Goutsi

A ceramic studio and art space that bridges the gap between traditional craft and contemporary aesthetics. The hands-on workshops inspire participants to explore their own creativity within the realm of ceramics.

→Papadiamantopoulou 6, 115 28
→21 0722 0450

F I L M

The Burglars, Henri Verneuil, 1971

Starring Jean-Paul Belmondo and Omar Sharif. Based on David Goodis' novel, it follows thieves in Greece pursued by a relentless detective. Tensions rise from external chases and internal betrayals. Noted for its car chases and Belmondo's daring stunts.

BARCELONA

“By day the old area of Barcelona is bustling, full of shouting, hammering, drilling and shutters being pulled up and down. You listen out for sounds. If you want a replacement gas cylinder you wait for the sound of the delivery man hitting a cylinder with a piece of metal in the street.”

Colm Tóibín

S E E

Nova Icaria beach

A popular beach among athletic locals who play beach volleyball here in the wind shadow of the long quay wall of the sports harbour. Also suitable for a safe swim, as two long breakwaters protect the sandy cove from high waves. Check out the seafood restaurants at the beachfront offering a classic Fideuà.

Walden 7

A social-housing experiment incorporating Ricardo Bofill's view on residential architecture. Its alien design, a vertical labyrinth over 16 stories with seven interconnecting interior courtyards is related to B.F. Skinner's science-fiction novel "Walden Two" in which he depicts a utopian community.

→Ctra. Reial, 106, 08960 Sant Just Desvern,
→33 71 80 63

Parc del Laberint d'Horta

Barcelona residents have been able to get lost in their own city since the turn of the 18th century—thanks to this garden maze designed by Italian engineer Domenico Bagutti. The city's oldest park, sitting on the Serra de Collserola hillside, is a feat of landscape gardening. It's worth the 25-minute subway trip from the centre.

→Passeig dels Castanyers, 1, 08035
→931 53 70 10

Mies van der Rohe Pavilion

The Mies van der Rohe Pavilion in Barcelona is an iconic modernist masterpiece. Designed by architect Ludwig Mies van der Rohe for the 1929 International Exposition, it embodies minimalist elegance with its sleek lines, glass walls, and travertine columns. A timeless example of architectural innovation and simplicity.

→Av. de Francesc Ferrer i Guàrdia, 7, 08038
→932 15 10 11

Parc de l'Espanya Industrial

Barcelona's most controversial park has a rich historical tapestry. Once a bustling industrial complex during the late 19th century, it housed the 1888 Universal Exposition, showcasing Spain's industrial prowess. The park's transformation began in 1985 when the architects Luis Peña Ganchegui and Francesc Rius turned it into a postmodernist masterpiece – a design route which a lot of locals still do not like much.

→Carrer de Muntadas, 1, 08014
→900 226 226

T A S T E

Ultramarinos Marín

Here, it's all about fresh seafood, sourced directly from fishing boats, cooked to perfection with simplicity, and minimal sauces. Chef Adrià Cartró Devide embodies this philosophy: the food is straightforward and honest, yet made with the finest ingredients. Even meat lovers will be delighted: the dishes are expertly grilled over a hot charcoal grill.

→C/ de Balmes, 187, 08006
→932 17 65 52

BARCELONA

Suculent

Behind the unassuming facade gastronomy transforms into an artful journey. With a menu rooted in Catalan tradition and elevated by contemporary flair, each dish is a harmonious dance of flavours and textures. The ambiance, a blend of rustic charm and modern sophistication, sets the stage for an unforgettable dining experience. From the meticulously crafted dishes to the attentive service.

→Rambla del Raval, 45, 08001
→934 43 65 79

Compartir

The little sibling of the famous Disfrutar presents a contemporary take on Catalan cuisine. The restaurant's shared dining concept and innovative menu offer an engaging gastronomic experience, reflecting the city's dynamic culinary scene.

→C/ de València, 225, 08007
→936 24 78 86

Cañete

Traditional Spanish cuisine with a twist at an informal but elegant restaurant: With a lively atmosphere and a menu based on locally sourced ingredients, this classic offers an authentic glimpse into Barcelona's vibrant food culture. The best seats are at the bar looking into the large polished open kitchen.

→Carrer de la Unió, 17, 08001
→932 70 34 58

Bar del Pla

This might look like just another traditional tapas joint. But chef Jordi Peris is taking old-school recipes and jazzing them up with a modern influence. Try his trotters with raisins and pine nuts, a juicy classic that will play on your tongue all the way home.

→C/ de Montcada, 2, 08003
→932 68 30 03

Entrepans Díaz

There are sandwiches all over the city, but here they offer them with a contemporary take. Think of bread specially delivered by the artisan baker Forn de Sant Josep and filled with such delectable things as crispy squid with squid-ink aioli. All of which pairs rather nicely with cocktails, wine or beer at any time of the day or night.

→C. de Pau Claris, 189, 08037
→934 15 75 82

Funky Bakers Eatery

The cute breakfast spot in Raval, crafts artisanal pastries and specialty coffee. With a focus on quality, locally sourced ingredients and an inviting, modern space, it offers a refreshing take on the traditional bakery experience.

→C. de Bailén, 61, 08009
→681 95 23 13

Berbena

An intimate eatery in the Gracia district with a thoughtfully curated menu. With a focus on seasonal and local ingredients, it offers an exploration of the new style of Catalan-inspired kitchen. Try the ox tongue gyoza.

→Carrer de Minerva, 6, 08006
→691 95 77 97

Batea

A seafood-centric spot in the Born neighbourhood, offers a dining experience rooted in Mediterranean culinary tradition. With its refined atmosphere and commitment to fresh, sustainably sourced produce, it offers a sophisticated culinary journey.

→Gran Via de les Corts Catalanes, 605, Pl. Baja, 08007
→934 06 87 92

Mont Bar

With the former head chef of Albert Adria's "Tickets" coming on board here, the wine bar added another layer of creative food to its roster. Expect dishes like "Chicken Skin Sandwich with Squid" and "Mild Smoked Tuna Ventresca with Pine Nut Vinaigrette" accompanying your bottle of Spanish wine.

→C/ de la Diputació, 220, 08011
→933 23 95 90

T O U C H

Mauri

Mauri is more than a traditional pastry shop – it is a beloved institution. With a commitment to artisanal baking techniques and high-quality ingredients, it offers a sweet slice of local culinary heritage.

→Rambla de Catalunya, 102, 08008
→932 15 10 20

Wah Wah Records

A vinyl collector's paradise. Situated in the center, this record store boasts an impressive array of musical treasures, spanning various genres from funk, jazz, experimental electronics, and psychedelia of all styles. The knowledgeable staff, led by owner Jordi Segura, also has a taste for obscure sounds - dive into a vinyl exploration.

→Carrer de la Riera Baixa, 14, 08001
→934 99 67 94

Moco Concept Store

A design-focused store that presents a carefully curated collection of contemporary furniture and home accessories, embodying the essence of Barcelona's distinct design sensibilities.

→C/ de Montcada, 27, 08003
→936 29 18 50

sivasdescalzo

A light-tower for the local streetwear scene. The shop offers a wide range of urban fashion and sneakers, offering a mix of both established brands and emerging designers.

→C. de Bailén, 18, 08010

Llibreria Ona

The new shop of Llibreria Ona offers a retreat for book lovers. Its carefully curated selection of Catalan literature, nestled in a characterful space with curated events, offers a dive into Barcelona's literary scene.

→C/ Gran de Gràcia, 217, 08012
→932 38 97 22

S M E L L

Razzmatazz

The flagship of Barcelona's clubs, featuring a spacious concert hall and five different clubs hosting diverse musical genres. So, it's better to take a look at the program to see what's on, but typically, all booked acts stand for a certain quality.

→C/ dels Almogàvers, 122, 08018
→933 20 82 00

BARCELONA

Bar Sauvage

This Born-based bar serves meticulously crafted cocktails in a laid-back atmosphere. Afterward, dance the night away in the intimate black light cave in the basement, accompanied by captivating Latin-infused sounds.

→Pg. del Born, 13, 08003
→938 32 51 84

Moog

This classic venue has been dedicated to various formats of electronic music for years – from minimal techno through to Detroit. The “mirror room” upstairs features more pop-oriented sets, while the bunker-style bottom floor is all about underground beats.

→C/ de l’Arc del Teatre, 3, 08002
→933 19 17 89

Macarena Club

Barcelona is no stranger to small clubs, but with an oft-met capacity of 80, this one takes the cake. Urban myths abound of stumbling in to find Richie Hawtin or Ricardo Villalobos in the midst of an unannounced set—which only adds to the allure of this tiniest of serious dance-music halls.

→Carrer Nou de Sant Francesc, 5, 08002
→933 01 30 64

Boadas Cocktails

This storied cocktail bar deserves a nicer sign than the one it currently sports, but once inside the atmosphere is pure 1930s. Comprised of a single room with wooden bar and panelling, it has a warm glow, as if seen through the bottom of a glass of amber liquid. Joan Miró and Ernest Hemingway both drank here and would still feel at home today, being served by attentive bar staff in full black tie.

→C/ dels Tallers, 1, 08001
→933 18 95 92

H E A R

F I L M

The Passenger, Michelangelo Antonioni, 1975

A weary journalist embarks on a transformative journey after assuming the identity of a recently deceased man. As he steps into the life of another, he is forced to confront his own disillusionment and disconnection from the world. This Michelangelo Antonioni film serves as a poignant exploration of identity and human nature.

SBAGLIATO
SECLUSION
SECLUSION
JACKFRUIT

BERLIN

"Paris is always Paris and Berlin is never Berlin!"

Jack Lang

S E E

Haus am Waldsee

It's worth taking the 30-minute train from downtown Berlin to visit this picturesque contemporary art space situated in a charming villa overlooking a lake. Expect a carefully curated selection of contemporary art and rotating exhibitions.

→Argentinische Allee 30, 14163
→030 8018935

KW Institute for Contemporary Art

Art galleries mushroomed in Mitte after the fall of the Wall. It was in an old margarine factory where a group of artists hatched this long-running space. Eschewing a permanent collection, they believe a changing programme allows the right responsiveness to an art world in flux.

The courtyard—complete with Dan Graham's glass-box-like bar—encapsulates the interactive ethos of the institution.

→Auguststraße 69, 10117
→030 2434590

Hansaviertel

Hansaviertel, a modernist housing project born from the Interbau architectural exhibition in 1957, represents Berlin's post-war architectural rejuvenation. Its diverse array of buildings designed by over 50 international architects – including names like Oscar Niemeyer, Arne Jacobsen or Alvar Aalto – provides a fascinating insight into the city's architectural evolution.

Neue Nationalgalerie

Reopened in 2021, the building itself, designed by Mies van der Rohe, is an icon of 20th-century architecture and now houses an impressive collection of modern art. Since 2022, Klaus Biesenbach, founder of KW and former director of LA's MOCA, has been in charge of the impressive program.

→Potsdamer Str. 50, 10785
→030 266424242

Strandbad Wannsee - Berliner Bäder

The lake is one of the largest urban inland swimming areas in Europe. Its famous sandy beach is packed with leisure seekers on warm days, and its island—a nature conservation area—can be reached by ferry. If you take a stroll on Pfaueninsel (Peacock Island), you'll see how it got its name.

→Wannseebadweg 25, 14129
→030 787322350

T A S T E

St. Bart

Nestled in the ambiance of a German Kneipe, this place represents the culinary confluence of German and British cuisines, offering seasonal dishes meant for sharing. Named after the apostle and patron of chefs, this dimly lit restaurant features a tiled exterior facade and serves up original dishes accompanied by beer and cocktails. Don't miss the popular Sunday roast!

→Graefestraße 71, 10967
→030 40751175

annelies

A breakfast favorite. But please don't expect modern standards like avocado toast or eggs benedict. Allow yourself to embrace new ideas such as sourdough toast with marinated mushrooms or French toast with strawberries and woodruff. Unfortunately, it's always quite crowded here.

→Görlitzer Str. 68, 10997

Restaurant Dóttir

The culinary embassy for Nordic cuisine: Icelandic Chef Victoria Eliasdóttir blends traditional Scandinavian fare with contemporary culinary techniques. Nestled within the new Hotel Chateau Royal, the decor and innovative menu provide a gastronomic journey that reflects the city's affection for art, tradition, and just a hint of decadence.

→Mittelstraße 41, 10117
→030 23456770

893 Ryōtei

Hidden from plain view: Behind its graffiti-adorned mirrored exterior, one wouldn't anticipate finding an elegant restaurant! Step inside to the black-themed interior with intimate tables, centered around an open kitchen. The host, Duc Ngu, is one of the innovators of the culinary scene in Berlin and operates numerous restaurants, particularly in Charlottenburg. This is our favourite: you'll uncover an intriguing Japanese culinary journey, enhanced by South American influences.

→Kantstraße 135/136, 10625
→0176 56754107

Bier's Kudamm 195

Traditional currywurst stand on Kurfürstendamm. At night, on the way home, quirky groups often gather here at the standing tables for sausage, beer, or piccolo. And: Consider beforehand whether you consume your currywurst with or without casing.

→Kurfürstendamm 195, 10707
→030 8818942

Paris Bar

A legendary hangout with a classic French kitchen and a good bet for an arty dinner between walls clustered with unique contemporary paintings. Many of them are by the famous Martin Kippenberger, who was broke most of the time and paid his bills with his work.

→Kantstraße 152, 10623
→030 3138052

Nobelhart & Schmutzig

Sommelier Billy Wagner and Micha Schäffer opened this spot in 2015 and their goal was not to fit in, but to break the rules of fine dining. Their motto "brutal lokal" sets the tone. No to lemons! No to chocolate! They don't even use pepper, because you can't source it locally. This radical restraint has been the catalyst for a new kind of Berlin cuisine

→Friedrichstraße 218, 10969
→030 25940610

Rogacki

Back in 1928, Rogacki started out with just smoked fish. Today, the market hall boasts over 70 species of fresh fish for you to prepare at home and also houses a few restaurant tables. From smoked eel to king prawns, traditional German classics sit beside international delicacies. Berliners often choose to combine their shopping with a lunch break.

→Wilmersdorfer Str. 145/46, 10585
→030 3438250

otto

After honing his skills at Maaemo in Oslo, Loco in Lisbon, and Noma in Mexico, chef Vadim Otto Ursus opened his own locale in Berlin where strictly local and seasonal organic products, wild plants and fruits come together extravagantly on the plate. Apart from a strong focus on fermentation and preservation, otto is also very dedicated to a zero-waste philosophy.

→Oderberger Str. 56, 10435
→030 58705176

Da Jia Le

The place offers an authentic culinary journey through the flavours of northeastern China, the Dongbei cuisine. Enriched by trade, migration, and historical connections, it embraces Korean, Mongolian, Japanese, and even Russian influences. Discover invigorating salads, delicate dumplings, tantalizing eggplant and tofu delicacies, and Chun Bing - akin to a Chinese burrito.

→Goebenstraße 23, 10783
→030 21459745

T O U C H

Andreas Murkudis

Concept-store king Andreas Murkudis is pushing the retail envelope with two shops on this street. AM is a 1,000 square-metre former newspaper building, redone in post-industrial chic and stocked with curated clothes, creams and design items. The stock includes well-knowns like Issey Miyake and Céline as well as collections from his brother Kostas.

→Potsdamer Str. 81, 10785
→030 680798306

The Store X Berlin

Berlin's upwardly mobile creative set have carved out a niche for themselves in Mitte's Soho House, and this ground-level boutique is all their consumerist dreams come true. From records and art books to clothes and accessories—think Mansur Gavriel, Christopher Kane, Kenzo, et al—there's everything for the modern cool girl or boy.

→Torstraße 1, 10119
→030 405044550

Voo Store

Tucked away in a beautiful courtyard off Oranienstrasse you'll find this super slick concept store, which focuses on high-end street-wear and trendy labels like Acne Studios, Marni, Vetements and Margiela. The offer is rounded out by a large collection of accessories, magazines and design objects, as well as in-house café Companion Coffee.

→Oranienstraße 24, 10999
→030 61651112

Markthalle Neun

This indoor food market offers a fresh selection of cheeses, meats and produce on a daily basis. The hit weekly "Street Food Thursdays" sees the city's finest food makers set up shop to sling food court-friendly versions of their star dishes.

→Eisenbahnstraße 42/43, 10997

do you read me?!

This hip and well-stocked magazine store offers an assortment of international press. The spectrum ranges from fashion, photography and art, through architecture, design, cultural matters and society.

→Auguststraße 28, 10117
→030 69549695

S M E L L

Sameheads

The intimate Lo-fi neon cave is a mesmerizing fusion of artistic expression, pulsating beats, and a wonderfully diverse crowd. This club goes beyond conventional Berlin (techno) nightlife norms, offering a dynamic musical lineup that spans Italo, Afro, Disco, Wave, and Latin sounds.

→Richardstraße 10, 12043
→030 70121060

Hard Wax

Hardwax is more than a record store and music distributor – it was and is the nucleus for the techno underground for over 30 years: Founded in 1989, it's the cornerstone of Berlin's scene – and meanwhile for a lot of visitors from all over the globe.

→Paul-Lincke-Ufer 44A, 10999
→030 61130111

OHM

This club is the little dirty sister of the legendary Tresor. It can be found on the same complex in the battery room of the former heating power plant. The location is known for its excellent sound system and for hosting emerging electronic music artists.

→Köpenicker Str. 70, 10179

Würgeengel

A laid-back blend of cocktail and dive bar makes for a great beginning as well as a concluding destination for the night. Ideal for mingling and getting to know people. By the way, the name is derived from Luis Buñuel's 1962 film "The Exterminating Angel."

→Dresdener Str. 122, 10999
→030 6155560

Heideglühen

A hidden gem in Berlin's club scene and likely one of the few places that still captures the vibe of the city's club scene in the 1990s. There is no fixed program or schedule, but be sure to explore the events hosted by Berlin's iconic DJ Woody, featuring international house DJs such as Chez Damier or Move D. The party typically kicks off in the afternoon and continues until the following morning.

→Seestraße 1, 13353

H E A R

F I L M

Menschen am Sonntag, Robert Siodmak, Edgar G. Ulmer, 1930

An avant-garde silent film that tells the tale of five Berliners spending their Sunday out and about in the city. The film, void of professional actors and showcasing scenes from ordinary life, provides a glimpse into Berlin during the Weimar Republic and is a testament to the human condition.

Coca-Cola
Coke

BRUSSELS

"In Brussels, everything is easy..."

Eric-Emmanuel Schmitt

S E E

Villa Empain

The estate was originally a private residence and now functions as a cultural center and exhibition venue. Constructed between 1930 and 1934 in the Art Deco style by architect Michel Polak, it was commissioned by Baron Louis Empain. The villa later saw use as an embassy before being reintroduced to the public in 2011.

→Av. Franklin Roosevelt 67, 1050
→02 627 52 30

Cauchie House

Steeped in history, this early 20th-century masterpiece is a treasure trove of Nouveau Art and is the residence of artist Paul Cauchie. Its intricate facades present a striking display of sgraffito, a nod to the artist's passion

for the technique.

→Rue des Francs 5, 1040
→0473 64 26 97

CBR Building

This landmark is an intriguing combination of the modern and the retro, designed by architect Constantin Brodzki. With its distinctive curved concrete window modules, the building is classified as a “New Brutalist” piece of architecture. Keep an eye out for public events or lectures that provide opportunities to explore the interior.

→Chau. de la Hulpe 185, 1170 Watermael-Boitsfort

Foundation Frison Horta (Private Museum)“A Living Museum”

Reflecting the genius of Victor Horta, this elegant townhouse-turned-cultural center hosts events designed to

bring art and architecture enthusiasts together. Explore its Art Nouveau roots and enjoy the intricate detailing characteristic of Horta's design philosophy.

→37 Rue Lebeau, Sablon, 1000 Brussel, Belgium
→02 330 47 96

Comics Art Museum

Offering a journey through the world of Belgian comics, this Center captures the essence of beloved characters like Tintin and Smurfs. Housed in a stunning Horta-designed building, it showcases the dynamic blend of fine art and storytelling.

→Rue des Sables 20, 1000
→02 219 19 80

T A S T E

Le 203

In this bistro kitchen, the chef primarily employs organic ingredients, crafting creative dishes with a Mediterranean touch. The attractively priced menu changes every Tuesday, reflecting the chef's inspiration. Reservations are not accepted, for evening visits, arrive before 7 pm.

→Chau. de Waterloo 203, 1060 Saint-Gilles, Belgium
→02 539 26 43

Le Tournant

The small restaurant welcomes you with the highly creative cuisine of chef Denis Delcampe who revives traditional Belgian cuisine. His eatery offers a rotating menu of seasonal ingredients that showcase local farm-to-table concepts.

→Chau. de Wavre 168, 1050 Ixelles, Belgium
→02 502 61 65

Chabrol Restaurant

This location delivers a dining experience inspired by traditional Parisian bistros. Savour authentic, flavorful dishes that reflect the simplicity and comfort of home-style French cuisine.

→Av. Louis Bertrand 61, 1030 Schaerbeek, Belgium
→02 463 13 04

KROKET

More than fast food: Providing a refreshing twist on Belgian comfort food, Kroket delights aficionados of artisanal croquettes – such as Croquette de Bacalhau or with Shiitake. Additionally, they present main dishes and a selection of six distinct beers to choose from.

→Rue Caroly 37, 1050 Ixelles, Belgium
→02 580 16 30

Tatar

Luca Termine artfully combines Mediterranean and Japanese influences, seamlessly mastering this fusion despite the geographical divide. His culinary ingenuity shines through in every dish he prepares, a skill honed during his debut at the renowned Japanese restaurant, Kamo. A seafood enthusiast, his diverse tartar creations are bound to captivate your palate.

→Rue de l'Aqueduc 155, 1050 Ixelles, Belgium
→02 647 09 04

seven brussels

Breakfast Choice: With its minimalist design, this contemporary all-day café offers homemade, seasonal breakfast options, complemented by specialty coffee. Ingredients are sourced from local, sustainable suppliers. Be aware that the use of laptops is restricted between 12 pm and 3 pm.

→Rue Edith Cavell 10, 1180 Uccle, Belgium

Restaurant Aster

The tasting menu at this recently opened establishment promises a gastronomic adventure from start to finish. Embracing a philosophy that celebrates the essence of the ingredients, the young culinary virtuoso Tubo Logier curates an exquisite experience, spotlighting local fish and vegetables meticulously prepared over an open flame. A vegetarian alternative is also available.

→Rue Antoine Dansaert 202, 1000

REBEL

A petite yet lively natural wine bar with a spirited cuisine. Founded by Paul-Antoine, the culinary innovator behind Ötap. The kitchen crafts a remarkable menu, extending until 2 am, creating a vibrant atmosphere where plates and stories are shared.

→Rue Lesbroussart 48, 1050 Ixelles, Belgium
→0471 90 34 66

Le Vismet

Located near the old fish market, this place is renowned for its fresh seafood offerings. From platters of fruits de mer to intricately plated mains, the menu is a homage to Belgium's coastal traditions.

→Pl. Sainte-Catherine 23, 1000
→02 218 85 45

L'Altitude

An audiophile bar with Art Deco elegance. A place where sonic enthusiasts can relish an auditory journey and share plates and a bottle of wine. They offer a diverse program, featuring monthly listening sessions and "guest diggers sessions".

→Av. Molière 2, 1190 Forest, Belgium
→02 414 46 66

T O U C H

Benoît Nihant Chocolatier

This artisan chocolate shop, helmed by master chocolatier Benoît Nihant, introduces you to the art of bean-to-bar chocolate-making. Explore the rich flavours of cacao sourced from around the globe.

→Chau. de Waterloo 506, 1050 Ixelles, Belgium
→02 534 81 00

Les Enfants d'Edouard

Step back in time at this high-end vintage store that showcases a finely curated selection of men's and women's clothing. The vast vast collection of more than 5,000 items from Azzedine Alaïa to Yohji Yamamoto is presented in a majestic mansion on two floors.

→Av. Louise 175, 1050
→02 640 42 45

Saint-Martin Bookshop

A bookshop for collectors: Delve into limited editions of artists' books, elusive catalogues showcasing modern and contemporary maestros, and a curated selection of art and fashion magazines. All housed within the iconic Maison Martin Margiela, exuding his unmistakable spirit.

→Rue de Flandre 114, 1000
→0487 13 65 72

Marché aux Puces

Known as a treasure trove for vintage and antique enthusiasts, this market is a celebration of Brussels' eclectic spirit. From early morning until afternoon, you can explore, haggle, and discover a variety of interesting finds.

→Pl. du Jeu de Balle 79, 1000

Via Antica

This three-floor antique shop is a paradise for antique lovers, filled with a mix of furniture, art, and decor from different eras. Its curated collections, ranging from Art Nouveau to Mid-century, inspire a sense of nostalgia and artistic appreciation.

→Rue Blaes 40, 1000
→02 503 50 64

S M E L L

Fuse

This club stands as an emblem of electronic music culture. With a legacy spanning decades since 1994, this iconic venue has magnetized the Belgian techno community. After temporarily losing its permission due to noise complaints in early 2023, reopened for an additional two years.

→Rue Blaes 208, 1000

BRUSSELS

Edgar’s Flavors

An easygoing cocktail establishment with a literary attitude: Inspired by his mother’s deep admiration for Edgar Allan Poe’s literary legacy, the French proprietor, Edgar, cultivates his devotion to mixology. His expertise shines through in the meticulous crafting of concoctions, often featuring agave spirits.

→Rue de la Concorde 63, 1000
→0493 38 81 96

C12

A young multidisciplinary hub, seamlessly merging the realms of art and clubbing – set in a shopping mall! Its commitment to inclusivity and diversity is reflected in its line-up of local and international performers like Lena Wilikens, Binh or Vera Mono.

→Rue du Marché Aux Herbes 116, 1000

Le Petit Lion

An authentic beer pub for every hour. Here, all walks of life come together for an affordable beer and to exchange stories. It’s often filled with a quirky mix of hipsters and elderly locals. It might not look like much, but it’s a local symbol.

→Rue Haute 232, 1000
→02 512 43 81

Kiosk Radio

Nestled in the historic Parc Royal, Kiosk Radio is an online radio platform, also hosting live DJ sets. The kiosk functions also as a unifying spot, where locals and visitors converge, creating an environment for individuals to relish music collectively – including vibrant open-air parties in summer.

→Pl. des Palais 10, 1000

H E A F

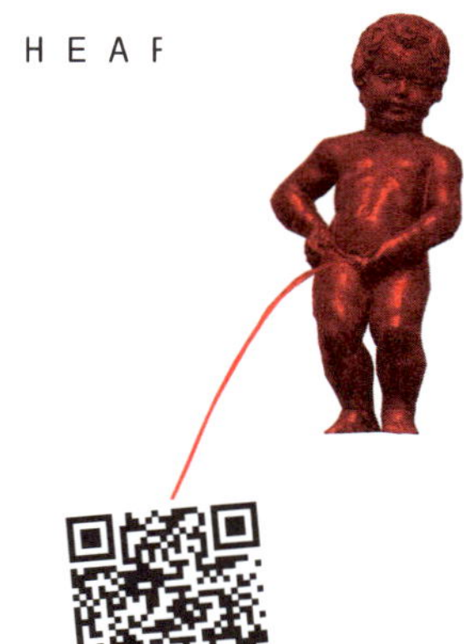

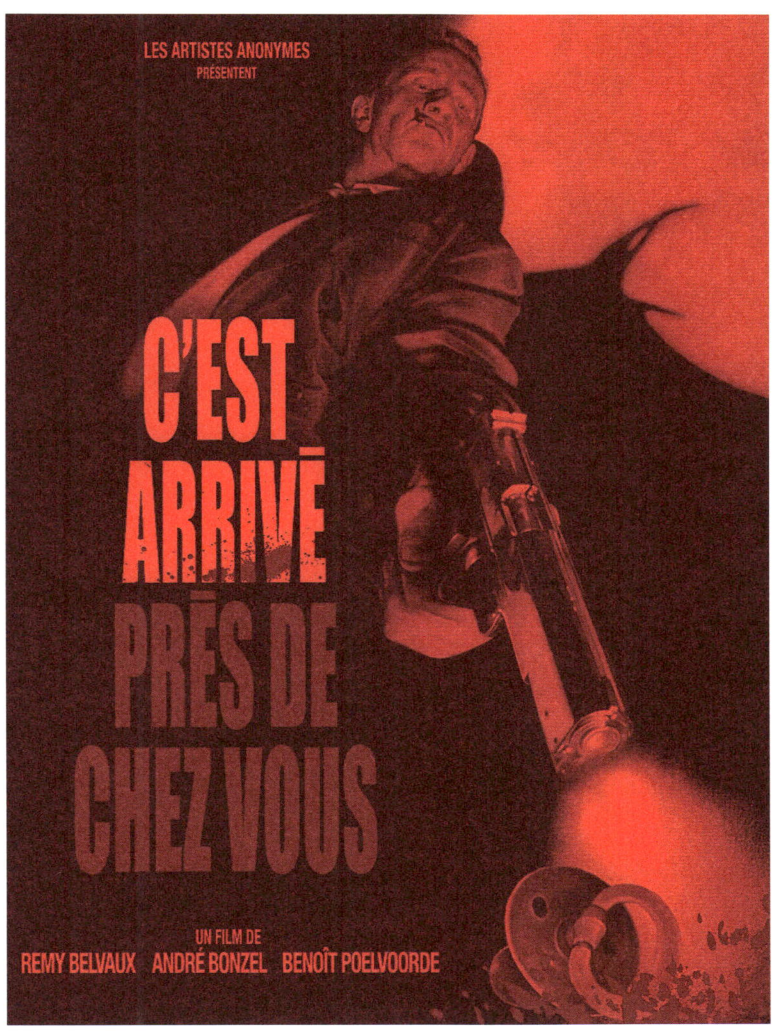

F I L M

Man Bites Dog, Rémy Belvaux, André Bonzel, Benoît Poelvoorde, 1992

A chilling black comedy and mockumentary that tells the story of a film crew following a ruthless serial killer. As they delve deeper into the disturbing, twisted psyche of the murderer, the lines between observer and participant begin to blur, leading to a shocking climax.

COPENHAGEN

“Copenhagen is a wet dream for lovers, cyclists, and people with a food fetish.”

Peter H. Fogtdal

S E E

Skovshoved

An architectural gem, the Skovshoved Petrol Station, was designed by Arne Jacobsen. Its iconic modernist structure stands as a testament to Copenhagen's deeply rooted culture of daily life design.

→Kystvejen 24, 2920 Charlottenlund, Denmark
→39 56 49 84

Louisiana Museum of Modern Art

Unveiled in 1958 by architectural minds Jørgen Bo and Vilhelm Wohlert, the museum's captivating design evolved with added wings and interconnected exhibition pavilions, linked by a glass corridor. At Louisiana, the structures and surroundings are artworks as much as the exhibitions they house, creating an immersive artistic experience.

→Strandvej 13, 3050 Humlebæk, Denmark
→49 19 07 19

Designmuseum Denmark

Showcasing Denmark's strong design legacy, their exhibitions cover many forms of design, including furniture, art, and fashion. Their permanent collection includes an incredible array of Danish furniture that will give you interior inspiration for the rest of your days.

→Bredgade 68, 1260
→33 18 56 56

Havnebadet Islands Brygge

Offering a refreshing urban beach experience in the heart of the city, Harbour Bath is the perfect spot to cool down in the summer. With crystal clear waters and architectural design, it's a symbol of Copenhagen's commitment to quality of life and sustainable urban development.

→Islands Brygge 14, 2300 København S, Denmark

Bredgade Kunsthandel

The town's oldest art dealer offers around seven annual exhibitions, They showcase contemporary art by both emerging and established artists from the Northern Atlantic region, with a diverse programme from glass sculptures to hyperrealistic paintings.

→Bredgade 69, 1260
→33 13 50 41

T A S T E

Slotskælderen Gitte Kik

The day-time restaurant offers a journey into Denmark's gastronomic tradition: featuring an array of smørrebrød (open-faced sandwiches) and boasting historic decor the whole atmosphere reflects the culinary heritage of the country.

→Fortunstræde 4, 1065
→33 11 15 37

Apollo Bar

Nestled within Kunsthal Charlottenborg, the daytime allrounder offers a fusion of museum café, bar, and restaurant. Adjacent, Apollo Kantine serves casual vegetarian lunches for students from the academy and everyone else.

→Nyhavn 2, 1051
→27 50 32 33

COPENHAGEN

Restaurant Barr

Housed in noma's old location, Barr is all about elevated comfort food. They focus on foods from the Northern Sea region, as well as on beer and aquavit as a complement to the food. Try the waffle; it's absurdly good.

→Strandgade 93, 1401
→32 96 32 93

Kødbyens Fiskebar

Located in a former market hall the restaurant serves up a culinary celebration of fish and seafood: With a commitment to sustainable fishing, simple recipes and high-quality ingredients. You can eat at the counter, on the sofas, or dine at a table, when the weather permits, also outside.

→Flæsketorvet 100, 1711
→32 15 56 56

Ticket

Under chefs Karlos Ponte and Henrik Dall's leadership, the place embarks on a gastronomic journey: The ever-evolving menu draws global inspiration, spanning Peru, India and Singapore, and presents a voyage of flavours through a tasting menu and à la carte selections.

→Otto Busses Vej 45
→30 20 40 79

Restaurant Koan

The 2 Michelin-starred restaurant using Korean flavours and techniques, melds the principles of Nordic and Asian cuisine. With a tasting menu that changes with the seasons, it provides an innovative dining experience that transcends borders.

→Langeliniekaj 5, 2100
→28 74 78 40

Kadeau

This restaurant focuses on food from the Danish island of Bornholm. It's a hyper-local concept, and it's been incredibly successful. The food and minimalist, raw interior are a perfect New Nordic marriage.

→Wildersgade 10B, 1408
→33 25 22 23

Juno the bakery

The hype is real! But also, really well-deserved. There is always a line snaking around the tiny little bakery and spilling onto the street, but it goes quickly so we recommend you wait it out. The fresh-baked breads are excellent (try the oat & honey!), but the real star is the cardamon bun.

→Århusgade 48, 2100

Ripotot

The quaint eatery unveils a daily evolving menu sourced from fields, farms, and seas. Crafting unique dishes with meats, fish, and vegetarian delights ensures a delectable experience catering to all palates.

→Store Kongensgade 56, 1264
→25 30 23 57

Kilden i haven, Tivoli

Experience chef Christian Hoffmann's modernized smørrebrød amidst lush greens for lunch, and evenings adorned with seasonal Danish gastronomy. He embodies Danish flavours while adding a touch of neighbouring delights like caviar and scallops.

→Vesterbrogade 3, 1553
→28 79 70 58

T O U C H

Time's Up Vintage

A treasure trove for vintage clothing lovers: With a curated selection of items dating from the 1920s to the 1980s, it's a testament to the city's vibrant fashion scene.

→Krystalgade 4, 1172
→33 32 39 30

Henrik Vibskov

Henrik Vibskov, an authority in fashion, music, and art, is celebrated as a creative virtuoso. His whimsical, abstract designs metamorphose everyday items – scarves, shirts, and trousers – into distinct artworks. Delve into his collections and explore other independent designers at his original store.

→Gammel Mønt 14, 1117
→33 14 61 00

ark books

The bookstore located in Nørrebro caters to a discerning clientele with its selection of Danish and international literature. With a focus on independent publishers, it offers a haven for book lovers.

→Møllegade 10, 2200

Conditori La Glace

More than a patisserie – it's a timeless sanctuary for decadent delights. Established in 1870, this patisserie retains its age-old charm, with the original mahogany, glass, and brass interior exuding a sense of nostalgia. Try the famous "Sport's Cake".

→Skoubogade 3, 1158
→33 14 46 46

Studio Oliver Gustav

Dive into the realm of intricate design aesthetics for art and furniture, where each piece carries its own story. Infused with a refined, dark allure, the collection mirrors the mind of its curator, an advocate for the compellingly minimal and profoundly tactile. Engage your senses with the masterful blend of avant-garde, rustic, and a touch of the arcane.

→Kastelsvej 18, 2100
→27 37 46 30

S M E L L

Duck and Cover - Cocktailbar

Owner Asper Riewe Henriksen's heritage infuses subterranean haven on Dannebrogsgade. Nostalgia blooms in the interior, a tribute to Henriksen's grandmother's home, invoking 1960s Copenhagen. The true stars are the cocktails, the bar's creativity and service earned it twin accolades at the 2017 Bartender's Choice Awards – akin to cocktail bar Oscars.

→Dannebrogsgade 6, 1660
→28 12 42 90

bird

"An intimate bar, where the melodic strains of vintage vinyl caress the space through handcrafted speakers. Equally important: exceptional cocktails. Not flashy, but crafted with expertise. Innovative, flawless flavour blends that captivate cocktail enthusiasts.

→Gl. Kongevej 102, 1850 Frederiksberg, Denmark
→30 48 11 02

Søhesten

From early evening till late, the bar radiates a cozy atmosphere, resonating with jazz and delectable libations. Tuesday quizzes offer snug nooks for revelry, while live jazz serenades Wednesdays and Thursdays from 8 pm.

→Sølvgade 103, 1307
→33 33 91 03

Baggen

There's usually a DJ or other live music happening at Baggen, one of the most popular nightclubs in the meatpacking district. This isn't about getting fancy; it's all cheap drinks and dancing your face off. It gets pretty crowded, but that's part of the fun right?

→Flæsketorvet 19, 1711

Culture Box

This local-favourite electronic music club has a few stages, bars, great live music from all over the world, and of course dancing dancing dancing. Please note that the opening hours listed here are for the Culture Box Bar, and the Red Box and Black Box are open at later hours, Friday and Saturday only. Closing hours are approximate; Culture Box closes when the show stops.

→Kronprinsessegade 54, 1306
→33 32 50 50

H E A R

F I L M

A Lesson In Love (1954) by Ingmar Bergman

Ingmar Bergman's "A Lesson in Love" is a delightful marital comedy that delves into the lives of a long-married couple seeking new romantic experiences. The film features a gynecologist who becomes infatuated with one of his patients, while his wife sets off to Copenhagen to rekindle an old affair with a sculptor. Skillfully blending scenes of lighthearted farce with periods of quiet introspection.

EDINBURGH

“My dear Sir, do not think that I blaspheme when I tell you that your great London, as compared to Dun-Edin, ‘mine own romantic town’, is as prose compared to poetry, or as a great rumbling, rambling, heavy Epic compared to a Lyric, brief, bright, clear, and vital as a flash of lightning”

Charlotte Bronte

S E E

National Galleries of Scotland: Modern One

Step into the evolution of 20th-century art at the Modern Two, where the collections span Surrealist and Dada works to contemporary pieces. Its intriguing exhibitions and the sculpture park offer engaging insights into modern art.

→75 Belford Rd
→0131 624 6200

Cramond Island

A tidal island in the River Forth, Cramond Island delivers a quiet retreat from city life. Accessible during low tide, it presents a different side of Edinburgh's natural landscape.

→Cramond Island EH4 6NU

Royal Botanic Garden Edinburg

Explore the city's green soul in the Royal Botanic Gardens. With diverse plant species from around the world, it's a serene haven for botany enthusiasts and nature lovers alike.

→Edinburgh EH3 5NZ
→0131 248 2909

Greyfriars Kirkyard

The cemetery is renowned for its historic graves but also for its ghost stories. The area is accessible during the day by special arrangement with the guides, and also at night by going on a City of the Dead Tour.

→26A Candlemaker Row

John Knox House

As one of the oldest buildings in Edinburgh, the John Knox House offers a peek into the life of the Scottish religious reformer. It serves as a reminder of the city's deep-seated history and religious heritage.

→43-45 High St
→0131 556 9579

Dulse

With a focus on Scottish seafood, the ground floor restaurant boasts an ever-evolving menu featuring shareable plates and fish delicacies. In the evening a basement wine bar presents an array of shared snacks, cured meats, cheeses, and selected wines.

→17 Queensferry Street
→0173 871 8387

Cafe Portrait

Located within the Scottish National Portrait Gallery, the place offers a delectable array of freshly sourced, locally inspired meals. Families will find a welcoming atmosphere, complemented by children's menus tailored to younger palates.

→1 Queen St
→0131 558 7031

Fishers In The City

This upscale seafood restaurant is set in an old converted warehouse in the heart of the city. It brings the fresh flavours of the Scottish coast to the city. Try the Pacific Rock Oysters from Loch Fyne - deli!

→58 Thistle St
→0131 225 5109

White Horse Oyster & Seafood Bar

Scotland is a seafood fan's heaven. Here, it comes with a creative twist - try the Crab Scotch Egg or the tempuras - and within a modernist setting. Oyster lovers: Happy Hour is weekdays between 12 pm and 4 pm.

→Royal Mile, 266 Canongate
→0131 629 5300

The Colonnades at the Signet Library

Indulge in afternoon tea within a historic library: Set within a Georgian edifice, the ambiance exudes grandeur with towering columns, expansive windows, and intricate embellishments. Elevating the experience is its culinary artistry: From the captivating amuse-bouche to the intricately designed cakes, each bite unveils meticulous craftsmanship.

→Parliament Square
→131 226 1064

tipo

The newest endeavour by the team behind Aizle and Noto embraces communal dining through an assortment of small and large plates, all within a minimalist wooden ambiance. Indulge in house-made pasta, exquisite cured meats, cheeses, and a distinct signature soft serve.

→110 Hanover St
→0131 226 4545

Timberyard

"Nestled within a 19th-century warehouse, the Michelin-starred family-run restaurant exudes rustic charm, complete with a wood burning stove and robust wooden tables. Skillfully curated, the menu seamlessly marries premium Scottish fish and meats with lesser-known botanicals like homegrown woodruff and sea buckthorn."

→10 Lady Lawson St
→0131 221 1222

Noto

Drawing inspiration from his experiences in New York, cheg and owner Stuart Ralston unveiled a captivating small plates haven. The establishment's enduring popularity is a testament to its allure. Meticulously crafted dishes showcase a global mosaic of influences, highlighting the flavours of Asia.

→47a Thistle St
→0131 241 8518

The Bon Vivant

You might mistake the place (only) for a whisky bar, with its low ceilings, candlelight and dark wood. Instead, it's a haven for appetites big or small. Main courses and lunch specials abound, but tapas-style "bites" offer small delicacies like duck liver parfait and ox tongue for the price of a gold coin.

→55 Thistle St
→0131 225 3275

The Edinburgh Larder

Craving a taste of tradition with a Scottish breakfast? Secure your spot in advance and relish Hash, Buttery Bap, Mushrooms on Toast, or Porridge. The morning feast is available all day long, with the added treat of a Bloody Mary kicking in from 11 AM onward.

→15 Blackfriars St
→0131 556 6922

T O U C H

Walker Slater Menswear

Classic tweed suiting, rugged country knits, formal shirts and casually dapper staple pieces are the dominating aesthetics here. Made from local fabrics and yarns, the whole range is set out in a store which has the appealing look of an old-school leather-and-tobacco men's club.

→16-20 Victoria St
→0131 220 9750

Valvona & Crolla

It is easy to hurry past this shopfront, unaware that within is Scotland's oldest Italian deli, a high-ceilinged space stacked to the rafters with an abundance of cheese, charcuterie, pasta and wine. Way at the back is a bookshop and cafe that's open all day serving dishes made from their own produce.

→19 Elm Row
→0131 556 6066

Bard Scotland

A captivating shop and gallery, an embodiment of Scottish craftsmanship. Founded by Hugo Macdonald and James Stevens, it weaves narratives of Scottish cultural heritage. The duo's vision: to elevate daily existence through craft, and to amplify the resonance of Scottish craft and design on the world stage.

→1 Customs Wharf, Leith
→0131 210 0106

Typewronger Books

Offering an array of eclectic titles, Typewronger Books is a haven for bibliophiles. Experience the joy of browsing through its thoughtfully curated selection and get lost in the world of words.

→4a Haddington Pl
→0131 556 5897

Cadenhead's Whisky Shop

The defining characteristic of this shop is the tang of whisky in the air, large quantities of which sit in the shop's own casks growing older and more delicious with each passing day. Buy direct from the casks or choose from a large range of bottles – a daunting task for the novice, but ask politely and advice will be forthcoming.

→172 Canongate
→0131 556 5864

S M E L L

Bramble Bar

This upscale speakeasy is hidden in the basement of a dry cleaners. It also caters to tastes in between neat nips of premium liquors and fancy cocktail concoctions, with the Bartenders' Choice menu. Try the bourbon with chinotto, vanilla chai cordial, tonic and angostura bitters for a refreshingly flavoursome pitstop.

→16A Queen St
→0131 226 6343

The Bow Bar

Offering a wide range of traditional ales and an impressive collection of Scotch whiskies, this bar is a classic local haunt. The ales are served from tall founts, a traditional Scottish method of dispensing that uses air and is now rarely seen. Seating is basic, so perhaps not a place you'll want to linger after a long, hard day, but ideal for a bracer.

→80 W Bow
→0131 226 7667

The Bongo Club

From drum and bass to techno, the club features residencies from some of Scotland's most notorious club nights. The location also serves as a cultural hub and is operated by an arts charity. Be sure to check out the Disco Makossa nights, a funk-filled trip through the sounds of African disco, kwaito, boogie, house and acid.

→66 Cowgate
→0131 558 8844

The Mash House

As a versatile music and events venue with three floors. The location is a key player in Edinburgh's nightlife with a diverse range from raves to live music events.

→37 Guthrie St
→0131 220 2514

Cabaret Voltaire

Short for Cabaret Voltaire, this subterranean club is an integral part of the city's underground music scene. Experience a blend of various styles in this unique cavernous setting with a warren of rooms and different types of music.

→36-38 Blair St
→0131 247 4704

H E A R

F I L M

Shallow Grave, Danny Boyle, 1994

Three friends discover their new flatmate dead with a suitcase full of money. This darkly comedic thriller, directed by Danny Boyle, explores the depths of greed and betrayal as the trio's actions set them on a path of destruction.

R
23
22
21
20
19
18
17
16
15
14
13

HAMBURG

"Hamburg totally wrecked us."

Paul McCartney

S E E

Deichtorhallen

Among the largest exhibition halls for contemporary art and especially photography in Europe, the Deichtorhallen are a visual highlight in themselves. The two historic buildings from 1911/13 impress with their open steel-glass architecture.

→Deichtorstraße 1-2, 20095
→040 321030

Oberhafen

A former railway repair yard turned creative quarter, houses artist studios, galleries, and eclectic dining spots. This urban space reflects the independent cultural pulse of the city.

→Oberhafen, 20457

Treppenviertel Blankenese

Treppenviertel, with its winding staircases and narrow lanes, offers captivating views of the Elbe River. The charming neighbourhood with colourful fisherman's houses, winding alleys and pretty villas, nestled in the hilly district of Blankenese, adds a Mediterranean flair to the Hanseatic city.

→Am Hang 9, 22587

Elbstrand

The Elbstrand, a riverfront beach, offers a tranquil respite within Hamburg's bustling cityscape. As an oasis of sand and pebbles, it provides a picturesque spot to watch ships sailing along the Elbe River.

→Elbstrand, 22605

U-Boot Museum Hamburg

Venture into maritime history. The museum offers a glimpse into life onboard one of the largest non-nuclear hunting and espionage submarines. The U-434 displayed served in the Russian Navy for 26 years until April 2002. It is one of the last submarines of the Tango class remaining globally.

→St. Pauli Fischmarkt 10, 20359
→040 32004934

T A S T E

Edmondo

An over-the-top ambiance reminiscent of a Wes Anderson film: inviting velvet seating, an opulent marble counter, and five-meter-tall shelves adorned with wines. Delighting patrons with expertly crafted Italian comfort cuisine spanning burrata, pizza, and pasta. And, don't forget to save room for dolce.

→Hohe Bleichen 17, 20354

Brücke 10

Experience the culinary spirit of Hamburg's harbour: This local favourite serves traditional, hearty fare in a setting that offers fantastic views of the city's bustling port. Don't miss out on the fish and crab sandwiches.

→St. Pauli-Landungsbrücken 10, 20359
→040 33399339

Restaurant Cox

In a Bistro-style setting, this classic restaurant presents a contemporary take on German cuisine, skillfully blending tradition with innovation. The establishment boasts a dedication to utilizing locally sourced ingredients to craft dishes that resonate with the changing seasons. The restaurant stands out for its exceedingly reasonable lunch specials.

→Lange Reihe 68, Greifswalder Str. 43, 20099
→040 249422

MAQUIS

Modern vegetable-focused creative cuisine takes center stage here. Johan Lindloff and Christian Piwitt serve vegetarian dishes that both surprise and delight. The ambiance oscillates between minimalistic and cozy.

→Thedestraße 2, 22767
→040 55619992

Kleine Brunnenstraße

On the agenda at this corner eatery with the nice summer terrace: refined North German cuisine that changes with the seasons. Their imaginative creations always prioritize fresh and high-quality ingredients. The Omakase-style surprise menu begins at just over 50 euros for 3 courses.

→Kleine Brunnenstraße, 22765

Restaurant Félix

A newcomer in Hamburg's bourgeois west, Chef Felix Bechtolf, who is half French, pays homage to his homeland. The preparation follows two directions: straightforward French bistro dishes or France-inspired creative cuisine – culinary craftsmanship with a personal twist. In the summer, they offer 50 outdoor seats.

→Rupertistraße 26, 22609
→040 53751921

Tigre

Xavi Lopez from Ecuador and Aurelio Moreno from Peru present their vibrant Latin American cuisine here. Dishes like ceviches are meant for sharing, accompanied by corresponding cocktails like Pisco Sour. The atmosphere is lively and diverse, making it perfect for a snack before a night of dancing.

→Nernstweg 32-34, 22765
→0176 22891575

Eier Carl

In the very spot where sailors once sought solace in eggnog a hundred years ago, today's global wanderers still find refuge. Nestled in Hamburg's maritime core, right by the Fish Market, this unassuming eatery serves up genuine local fare such as "Senfeier", "Labskaus", and "Pannfisch".

→Fischmarkt 3, 22767
→040 31977327

Teikei Café

A café where beans sail to Germany 100% climate-friendly, coupled with an exclusive use of seasonal, regional, and organic-certified ingredients, this daytime eatery stands as one of the city's most sustainable cafes. Plus: Owner Aaron's baking skills are equally commendable.

→Marktstraße 25, 20357

T O U C H

Herr von Eden

Reflecting the city's sharp sartorial style, Herr von Eden designs exquisite, bespoke suits. His first boutique showcases the city's flair for fashion and a dedication to exceptional craftsmanship.

→Marktstraße 33, 20357
→040 65065200

Walther Eisenberg der Mützenmacher

Step back into history at this traditional hat maker's shop. Since 1892 this shop has provided finely crafted hats. A selection of classic Mariner's caps awaits you, such as the Elbsegler ("Elbe sailor") and the Prinz Henry cap.

→Steinstraße 21, 20095
→040 335703

The Vintage Store

A haven for Midcentury design classics, with a prominent emphasis on Scandinavian design. The collection includes renowned brands such as Sika Møbler, Vamo, and Danish Control, as well as Italian classics from B&B Italia and Poltronova. Ideal for global visitors, worldwide shipping services are accessible.

→Goernestraße 17, 20249
→040 32539908

Flohmarkt Flohschanze

Experience the vibrant history of Hamburg at this popular Saturday flea market. Delve into a world of antiques, vintage fashion, and secondhand treasures – the pros arrive early before 8 am when it officially starts.

→Neuer Kamp 30, 20357
→040 2702766

Allike Store

This modern multibrand store is a dream for sneaker enthusiasts. Allike offers a curated selection of international brands and limited editions, reflecting the city's passion for urban styles.

→Virchowstraße 2, 22767
→040 38904116

S M E L L

Central Congress

Hardly recognizable as a bar from the outside. The interior design, inspired by the 1960s era, with wood veneer, leather armchairs, and a table arrangement resembling a conference room, is truly unique. It's also a place for serious drinking and – still – smoking.

→Steinstraße 5-7, 20095

Golden Pudel Club

Golden Pudel Club is the iconic club for music lovers in the city. Located by the Elbe River, it hosts a diverse array of music events but is always dedicated to quality and experience.

→St. Pauli Fischmarkt 27, 20359
→040 28468911

Waagenbau

This underground club is famous for its electrifying electronic music, curated by a mix of local and international DJs. With heart-pounding beats that surpass 120 BPM, it guarantees ecstatic nights under the strobe lights.

→Max-Brauer-Allee 204, 22769

The Chug Club

Tequila has never been more astonishing! This bar is a "Kiez" classic, offering distinctive and unique tequila flavours. Each small glass takes you on a journey of surprising taste combinations.

→Taubenstraße 13, 20359
→040 35735130

Mojo Club

The first Mojo parties took place in 1989. The club became an extension of the London acid jazz scene. Even today, the passion of the bookers lies in funk, soul, and jazz, but the live and DJ program occasionally ventures into commercial avenues – so make sure to check the schedule.

→Reeperbahn 1, 20359
→040 3191999

H E A R

F I L M

Rocker, Klaus Lemke, 1972

The raw depiction of 1970s Hamburg's rocker scene, portraying an intense, violent, and anarchic lifestyle. The movie, an integral part of New German Cinema, showcases non-professional actors embodying their real-life roles.

IBIZA

“The most virgin landscape I’ve ever encountered.”

Walter Benjamin

S E E

Sa Pedrera de Cala D’Hort

Some say it was a Phoenician quarry, others that it provided sandstone for Ibiza’s walls in the 16th century. Whatever its origins, carved gods and monsters testify to Sa Pedrera de Cala d’Hort’s discovery by hippies in the 1960s who named it Atlantis. Today it’s a spectacular trip for those in shape enough to make it back up.

→Sant Josep de sa Talaia, 07839

Paradise Lost

During the Christian invasion in 1235, the Moors escaped the Old Town of Ibiza across the island to Cap d’Albarca. There, they set up their new home – and this time they built a wall around it. Like a smaller, Ibizan equivalent to the Great Wall, the wall’s remains set the scenery for a

beautiful walk.

→Carrer del Passadís, 14, 07800
→627 58 92 05

Agua Blanca

An enchanting beach on Ibiza's north coast, offers clear waters and a peaceful atmosphere. Framed by cliffside forests, it provides a picturesque spot to soak up the Mediterranean sun.

→Agua Blanca, 07811

Aquabus Jet

When you ask some pros what the best thing about Ibiza is, they'll answer: the ferry to Formentera. That might sound extreme, but for those with time, visiting the small island sibling is a must due to its fine sandy beaches with

turquoise water and the off-season hippie vibe.

→Estación Marítima Ibiza - Formentera. Puerto de, 07800
→644 28 44 96

Museu Puget

Museo Puget showcases the works of Ibicencan painters Puget Viñas and Puget Riquer. The museum, housed in a traditional 18th-century house, offers a dive into the island's artistic legacy.

→Carrer Major, 18, 07800
→971 39 21 47

T A S T E

Bistro Mondo

Having honed his skills as an ex-sous chef at Noma (Copenhagen), Boris Buono now commands 'Taller de Sa Penya' and the 'Ibiza Food Studio,' his own restaurants, for several years. This year marks the unveiling of 'Bistro Mondo,' his latest venture located within the boutique hotel Gare du Nord, nestled in the lush, tranquil north of Ibiza."

→Carrer de sa Cala, 11, 07810
→697 34 57 91

Restaurant Camí de Balàfia

A Mecca for meat—grilled over carob, almond and olive wood and served in an exquisite foliage-covered courtyard. Run by the Marí family for decades, Balafia's chips are hand-peeled by the grandfather and the tomato salad is legendary. No cards, no menu, no prices in advance—just have faith in the quality

→Lugar, Carrer Venda de Balafia de Dalt, 25, 07812
→971 32 50 19

Cas Pagès

No reservations might mean a wait for a seat in the tree-sheltered garden. Consider this time to prepare your appetite for gigantic portions of coal-grilled beef and wood-cooked lamb. For local flavours try the "arroz matanza" – a soupy pork and chicken paella – or "sofrit pagès", a spicy sausage stew.

→Ctra. San Carlos, km 10, 07840 Santa Eulària des Riu,
→Illes Balears, Spain 971 31 90 29

La Paloma

Surrounded by breathtaking campo, this reconverted finca serves organic Mediterranean dishes with ingredients mainly sourced from its own garden and friends' farms. Kids are welcome and the evenings can turn into musical affairs.

→Carrer Can Pou, 4, 07812
→971 32 55 43

Taller Sa Peña by Ibiza Food Studio

Nestled within the enchanting streets of Ibiza's Old Town, this restaurant serves as the mothership for bespoke Ibiza Food Studio. Only the finest produce graces diners' tables, ensuring an authentic and top-notch dining experience influenced by the island's terroir – akin to a 5-star dinner at a friend's home."

→Carrer Alt, 2, 07800 Eivissa, Illes Balears, Spain
→628 85 46 54

Can Pilot

The star at this traditional grill restaurant is a kilo or more of t-bone ox steak finished at your table. The cool interior buzzes for lunch and the terrace is perfect for a star-gazing dinner.

→Avinguda Isidor Macabich, BAJO (CTRA, 07800 Sant Rafel
→971 19 82 93

El Zaguán

Nestled in the charming town of Ibiza, the place is known for its tapas. The quality of the well-priced food in this vibrant location is proven by the presence of local families.

→Av. de Bartomeu de Roselló, 15, 07800
→971 19 28 82

Can Jordi Blues Station

Savor a Thursday evening of live blues and rock at Can Jurdi. This venue, featuring intimate performances and drawing in locals and international residents alike, unites music enthusiasts and free thinkers beneath the starry Ibiza sky. By the next day, it transforms again into a friendly coffee and bar spot along the road for the islanders.

→Diseminado Jordi, 8773, 07830
→971 80 01 82

Boodiou

The tapas and cocktail bar is a hidden gem amidst the bustling tourist spots in Old Town. The place boasts vintage French decor, combining flair and pop art. With limited indoor seating, the sidewalk tables are perfect for people-watching.

→Carrer de la Mare de Déu, 10, 07800
→689 76 33 46

El Bigotes - Bullit

A highlight from the traditional Balearic kitchen is the “bullit de peix”, a fish and potato stew. Here it comes at late lunchtime with ocean views and in a rustic atmosphere.

→Camino Cala Boix a Cala Mastella, 138T, 07850
→650 79 76 33

T O U C H

Mercat De Forada

A local market trading mostly in produce, wines, fresh breads and baked sweets. You’ll also find a fine selection of natural health products. The market provides a vibrant snapshot of Ibiza’s commitment to sustainable living and local craftsmanship.

→PMV-812-1, 22, 07820
→670 34 03 56

L.A. STUDIO IBIZA

Fanny's iconic vintage clothing store in Ibiza Town offers a carefully selected range of retro pieces. The store's distinctive Ibizan bohemian flair appeals to the island's fashion-forward visitors - quirky, colourful, and sexy.

→C/ de Miquel Caietà Soler, 5-7 07800
→692 72 46 35

Can Cristofol Farm and Shop

A slice of Ibiza's agricultural bounty. This local farm shop offers fresh produce and artisanal goods, showcasing the island's commitment to sustainable farming practices.

→Poligon 1, Parroquia de, Venda de Morna, Disseminat, 37
→07850 610 63 71 55

Antonioli

The owner brings international cutting-edge fashion to Ibiza. Offering a curated selection of avant-garde brands, this boutique reflects the island's stylish, fashion-forward sensibilities.

→Carrer de Cas Dominguets, 17c, 07800
→871 11 06 31

Bomé

In their artisanal atelier, Dario since 1975 and lately his daughter Paloma craft unique leather goods. With decades of experience, Dario is the master designer, while Paloma is emerging with her own collections. Using premium vegetable-tanned leather, each piece is meticulously handmade, resulting in distinctive, one-of-a-kind creations.

→Calle de la Iglesia, numero 10, 07815
→646 84 34 01

S M E L L

Underground Ibiza

This stronghold of underground club culture draws locals for their typical after-work caña. The door policy can be touch and go. Nights at "el Under" alternate between laid-back and throbbing—thanks to a rotating cast of DJs, eager to play alongside owner Juanito.

→Diseminado Cas Arabins, 96, 07816
→971 19 86 56

Bar 1805

Punctuate a stroll through the labyrinthine alleys of D'alt Vila with a stop at this hidden terrace. French-style comfort food is accompanied by a slick selection of cocktails - all created by owner and mixmaster Charles. Come for the moules frites, stay for the absinthe drip - Charles offers it to anyone presenting themselves at the bar with a "real" anchor tattoo.

→Carrer Santa Llúcia, 7, 07800
→651 62 59 72

Pikes Ibiza

Attached to the hotel, the dance events with gigs from legends like DJ Harvey draw in a Brit-heavy crowd and are much loved by year-round islanders. They do real drinks and on a Sunday it's all served by the pool. Also, they're known to do wild theme nights.

→Camí de Sa Vorera, S/N, 07820
→971 34 22 22

Paradise Lost

Step into a world of crafted cocktails at Paradise Lost. This cozy bar, with its vintage decor and enticing drinks menu, offers a more laid-back side to Ibiza's nightlife.

→Carrer del Passadís, 14, 07800
→627 58 92 05

Bar Anita

An institution—plus a literal home address for some Ibizan locals. Since the 1960s it's been a favourite with artists, writers and hippies, who would trade work for drink and tapas. The house-made local liquor hierbas ibiçencas is perhaps the best on the island.

→Lugar Barri San Carlos, s/n, Islas, 07850
→971 33 50 90

H E A R

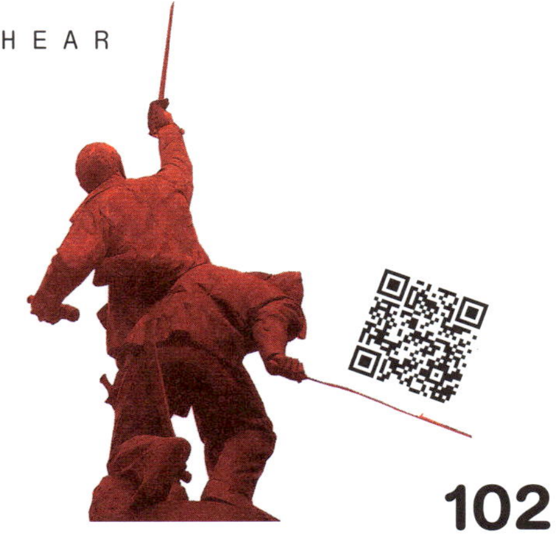

F I L M

F For Fake, Orson Welles, 1973

This inventive docudrama by Orson Welles delves into the world of illusion, forgery, and duplicity. It presents the stories of notorious fakers while exploring the blurred lines between art and deception, authenticity and pretense.

ISTANBUL

“Yesterday I looked upon you from a peak, sacred Istanbul... Falling in love with even your smallest neighbourhood is worth a whole lifetime.”

Yahya Kemal Beyatli

S E E

Gülhane Park

The serene urban oasis offers a beautiful display of seasonal flowers and provides stunning views of the Bosphorus. A quiet stroll here evokes Istanbul's past as a royal garden.

→Cankurtaran, Kennedy Cad., 34122

Sakıp Sabancı Müzesi

The historical two-story building on the shores of the Bosphorus belonged to several high-ranking Pashas from 1848. Businessman and philanthropist Sakıp Sabancı transformed it into a museum, showcasing his collection of Islamic art and Ottoman Empire paintings.

→Emirgan, Sakıp Sabancı Müzesi, 34467

Çamlıca Mosque

This modern and majestic mosque, situated on Istanbul's highest hill, presents breathtaking views of the city and the Bosphorus. Its intricate architecture was envisioned by the female architects Bahar Mızrak and Hayriye Gül Totu. Turkey's largest mosque, which opened in 2019, stands as a testament to their design prowess.

→Ferah, Ferah Yolu Sk. No:6 D:3, 34692

Ortakoy Pazar

Located in the upscale Ortakoy neighbourhood, this market ranks among the city's famed "high society markets." Unlike its counterparts, it exudes a more laid-back yet refined atmosphere, especially in its elegant clothing and accessory offerings. Though somewhat discreet, this intimate gem also provides stands for a delightful lunch break once discovered.

→Mecidiye, Mecidiye Köprüsü Sk. No:15, 34347

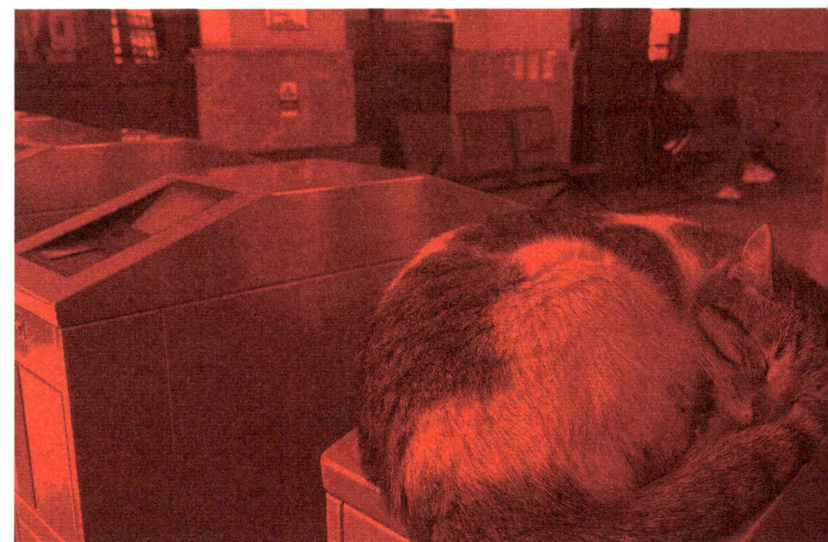

Burgaz Island

The tranquil Burgaz Island, just a brief ferry ride away from Istanbul and among the lesser crowded Princess Islands, provides a serene escape from urban life. Wander through its charming streets, and local eateries, and relish the stunning seaside vistas.

→Burgaz Island, Burgazadası, 34975

T A S T E

Yeni Lokanta

Like most metropolises, Istanbul's food scene is a fickle one. Chef Civan Er's restaurant has, however, prevailed – it continues to redefine modern Turkish cuisine. Tasting menu or a la carte, everything from the homemade bread and butter to the mantı (small dumplings with a yogurt and sumac sauce) to the grilled octopus are memorably delicious.

→Tomtom, Kumbaracı Ykş. No:66/B, 34433 Beyoğlu/İstanbul, Türkiye
→(0212) 292 25 50

Smelt & Co.

One day a Turkish chef, who used to work at Noma Copenhagen, and his partner decided that the endearingly dilapidated historic Balat neighborhood was the perfect place to open a tiny bistro. And so Smelt & Co. was born with its homemade kombucha mixes and cocktails and experimental dishes like artichoke tangine or minced salmon.

→Balat, Kiremit Cd. No:16/A, 34087
→538 286 54 65

Alaf

There was nothing particularly glamorous about Turkish street food until the chefs of Alaf came along and made it gourmet. Classics like kokoreç (chopped lamb intestines), işkembe (tripe soup) or uykuluk (sweetbread) are enhanced through quality ingredients and presentation.

→Kuruçeşme, Kuruçeşme Cd. No:19, 34345
→0532 015 94 19

Yakup2

Savor traditional meze and local delicacies in a vibrant ambiance. The diverse menu boasts a wide array of meze dishes, from timeless favorites like fava, hummus, and girit meze, to enticing seafood choices such as calamari and shrimp casserole. This captures the essence of an authentic dining adventure.

→Asmalı Mescit, Asmalı Mescit Cd. No:21 D:B, 34430
→(0212) 249 29 25

Balat Sahil

Only a few true meyhane lovers spend their evenings in Balat, basking in the nostalgia of this very classic restaurant. Above par dishes include marinated seabream, stuffed onions, Sinop-style liver and a rather legendary grilled turbot, which all pair well with many glasses of cold rakı.

→Balat, Mürselpaşa Cd. No:245, 34087
→(0212) 525 61 85

Koço

A classic meyhane that's been around since 1928, Koço is a real Kadıköy establishment. In the summer the tables outside are always fully booked as locals eat meze and drink rakı with a sea view. Random fact: the restaurant has a Greek Orthodox shrine and sacred spring in the basement.

→Caferağa, Moda Cd. No:171, 34710
→(0216) 336 07 95

Moda Aile Çay Bahçesi

Immerse yourself in local culture at this tea garden, where you can relish traditional Turkish tea. With its seaside setting, extensive tea choices, and delectable pastries, it's the perfect place for a relaxed interlude among locals.

→Caferağa, Park İçi Yolu, 34710
→(0216) 337 99 86

Neolokal

One of Istanbul's most experimental chefs, Mahsut Aşkar is adamant about preserving tradition. His dishes arrive like works of abstract art, bringing together the bounties of Mother Earth, endangered heritage foods and traditional Turkish recipes that are on the brink of being forgotten.

→Arapcamii Mahı, Bankalar Cd. No:11, 34420, 34421
→0551 447 45 45

Barba Vasilis

In the Ottoman Empire, the majority of meyhane proprietors were Greek-speaking Christians, known as 'Rums,' often referred to as 'Barba' or uncle. Barba Vasilis is an authentic Greek taverna offering classic dishes to share within a jovial setting.

→Yavuz Sultan Selim, Abdülezelpaşa Cd. no:97, 34083
→0531 947 93 93

Yanyalı Fehmi Lokantası

If you're a regular at Kadıköy's beloved fish market, Yanyalı Fehmi Lokantası won't be unfamiliar. Established in 1919 within the market, it continues its legacy by offering a rich selection of over 100 exquisite Turkish and Ottoman delicacies. Don't miss their unique meatballs enveloped in delicate eggplant slices.

→Osmanağa, Güneşli Bahçe Sok No:1, 34714
→(0216) 336 33 33

T O U C H

Sudietuz

The local designer brand, Sudietuz showcases prêt-a-couture collections and has achieved success through conceptual fashion design, distinguished by innovative fabrics. Their "street couture" with a contemporary flair is presented in a store that also serves as an atelier and showroom – simply ring the bell.

→53/A, Teşvikiye, Prf. Dr. Orhan Ersek Sk., 34365
→(0212) 246 68 75

shopi go

Turkey's first online concept shop launched in 2012 and has been expanding ever since. Its brick-and-mortar headquarters carry the contemporary brands and luxury streetwear collections that have made it a household name among the cool kids. You'll find Comme des Garçons, Marc Jacobs, Wood Wood and many more.

→Teşvikiye, Ahmet Fetgari Sk No:62, 34365
→444 8 684

Midnight Express

Explore a lavish concept store showcasing clothing, accessories, and home designs. Meticulously curated, the collection showcases the finest designers from Turkey and the Middle East. Don't miss Selim Mouzannar's jewelry or the pottery of Gülsüm Üzel and Ayşe Tanman.

→Bebek, Küçük Bebek Cd. No:3/b, 34342
→(0212) 263 21 11

Hole Academie

Founded by Didem Soydan and Umut Eker, this small independent concept store thrives on their enduring friendship. Geared toward the style-confident influenced by street fashion and subcultures, it seamlessly merges comfort with cutting-edge fashion. The store also offers bespoke jewelry.

→Teşvikiye, Osman F. Seden Sk. 7a, 34365
→0539 465 01 16

Begüm Khan

Begüm Khan offers statement pieces that celebrate Ottoman artisanship. Each meticulously crafted piece reflects Istanbul's rich cultural heritage infused with contemporary design elements.

→Harbiye, Mim Kemal Öke Cd. 14/3, 34367
→0538 023 04 38

S M E L L

Tavern

The small location serves up some excellent cocktails during the evenings accompanied by DJ music and plenty of unencumbered dancing. During dinner, things are a bit more low-key with tavern-style street food and meze.

→Firuzağa, A, Hayriye Cd. No:16/A, 34425
→0544 252 00 62

Sortie

This classic commercial club caters to diverse tastes, offering sunset afterworks and lively dance nights. The highlight is its breathtaking Bosphorus view. When night falls, it offers the full package: DJs, cocktails, dancers. Prices are upscale, and classier attire is recommended.

→Kuruçeşme, Muallim Naci Cd. No:54, 34345
→(0212) 327 85 85

Arka Oda

Anyone who's anyone in Kadıköy has spent an evening in Arkaoda, drinking in the back terrace and dancing to a local musician in the living room. A real hipster paradise famous for its illustrated monthly event calendars, Arkaoda even opened up in Berlin to an equally loyal fan base.

→Caferağa, Kadife Sk. No:18/A, 34710
→(0216) 418 02 77

BİNA

The Arkaoda team decided to take over a whole building to open their second drinking venue. Lounging areas on two separate floors and a large bar area with its own courtyard and fountain compose Bina, probably one the coolest places to hang out in Kadıköy at night.

→Caferağa, Kadife Sk. No:26, 34710
→(0216) 330 84 66

Klein phönix

A rising star in the city's nightlife scene. This versatile venue presents a fusion of musical genres, making it a must-visit for diverse tastes. Explore their schedule to find your perfect groove.

→Maslak, Atatürk Sanayi Sitesi 1. Kısım 43. Sk. 52. Sokak, 34385

H E A R

F I L M

James Baldwin: From Another Place, Sedat Pakay, 1973

Shot in Istanbul, Turkey, where Baldwin was living and writing, the film details the author talking about living abroad, the black experience in America, and his controversial private life.

LISBON

"From Alfama's arms to Liberdade
Paper lanterns, falling embers
Quiet cantors sing of saudade
The ever-twilight amber of your alleyways
Paint the air of evening so well
And strolls about the river bank
Suggest there's history left to tell."

Melody Gardot

S E E

Panorâmico de Monsanto

Perched high in Monsanto Forest Park, Panorâmico de Monsanto provides spectacular views of Lisbon. Once an upscale restaurant, it's now an abandoned yet intriguing spot that's been reclaimed by urban explorers and local artists.

→Estr. da Bela Vista, 1500

Furnas do Guincho

Set atop a cliff overlooking the Atlantic, Furnas is your best bet for lunch in Guincho. Sit down, breathe in the sea air, and order up a plate of arroz de marisco, Portugal's answer to paella.

→Guincho, 2750-642 Cascais
→21 486 9243

Calouste Gulbenkian Museum

Armenian oil magnate Calouste Gulbenkian bequeathed his collection to Portugal, and the selection covers East to West and antiquity to the Old Masters and Impressionists. For a more local flavour, the Gulbenkian-owned Modern Art Centre is just the opposite, with plenty of Portuguese works. Both are sited in the same expansive park, peppered with sculptures.

→Av. de Berna 45A, 1067-001
→21 782 3000

Atelier-Museum Júlio Pomar

Tucked down an anonymous alleyway, this gallery space explores the work of one of the country's most important artists. Pomar has worked over seven decades through many different phases. As a "neorealist" painter he was a vocal opponent of the Salazar regime in the 1940s.

→R. Vale 7, 1200-317
→21 588 0793

B.Leza

The main attractions at this cultural center are live music by travelling African bands and frenetic dance sessions, with an emphasis on Cape Verdean rhythms. Make it your first stop on a night out dedicated to reverse cultural colonialism.

→Cais Gás 1, 1200-161
→21 010 6837

T A S T E

O Palácio

If you're looking for a marisqueira with a rustic and local charm, this is your place. The main room is illuminated by neon lights, where a TV often airs soccer games. The guests mainly hail from the neighbourhood, ranging from large family gatherings to elderly individuals who enjoy reading while savouring fresh seafood or indulging in a Bifana afterwards.

→Rua Prior do Crato 142, 1350-263
→21 396 1647

Zé da Mouraria

It only serves lunch and it's likely to be packed—but it's well worth the wait. It's one of the most charismatic restaurants in the area and a great example of how tasty and diverse traditional Portuguese gastronomy can be. Go for the "bacalhau assado"—codfish grilled over a charcoal barbecue

→R. João do Outeiro 24, 1100-292
→21 886 5436

Gambrinus

Opened in 1936, with an interior untouched since 1964, these rooms breathe history. The quality of classics like "Sopa Rica de Peix" (fish stew) is as high as the prices. You can always avoid the main room, with its monumental granite fireplace, and go for a beer and an affordable steak sandwich at the informal bar.

→R. das Portas de Santo Antão 23, 1150-264
→21 342 1466

Palácio dos Duques de Lafões ou do Grilo

This magnificent neoclassical mansion, adorned with lush gardens and exquisite frescoes, has been transformed into a restaurant. The incredibly captivating ambiance of the three guest rooms is complemented by surrealistic performances during dinner. The kitchen is focused on high-quality ingredients and infused with a creative touch.

→Calçada do Duque de Lafões 1, 1950-207
→910 440 942

Cervejaria Ramiro

The more popular the restaurant, the fresher the seafood—that's the rule of thumb in Lisbon. If you take a look at the daily queues here, it should be an obvious choice.

→Av. Alm. Reis 1 H, 1150-007
→969 839 472

Belcanto

José Avillez launched a new generation of Portuguese cuisine with his groundbreaking restaurant and two-Michelin-star kitchen. Enjoy avant-garde creations like the "olive trilogy", a piece of fish made to look like a Jackson Pollock painting, and other personality-rich creations.

→R. Serpa Pinto 10A, 1200-026
→21 342 0607

Boavista Social Club

Grab a small bite, savor natural wines, and step out for a dance later. This unique hybrid venue is also renowned for its lively musical events. Its urban ambiance, paired with a diverse music scene, renders it a favoured destination for the city's young and trendy crowd.

→Rua da Boavista 16, 1200-275

Sea Me Peixaria Moderna

What happens when Japanese and Portuguese cuisines come together? Answer: you get a menu featuring taste sensations like the Azores parrot fish and tuna with wasabi ice cream.

→Rua do Loreto 21, 1200-241
→21 346 1564

Cacué

A cozy Lisbon gem with an inviting atmosphere and attentive service. Off the tourist path, it's perfect for escaping crowds. The menu features traditional Portuguese dishes with modern flair, including seafood delights like razor clam rice and scarlet prawn rice, as well as meat options.

→R. Tomás Ribeiro 93 C, 1050-227
→934 553 494

Café No Chiado

An enduring downtown favourite. On the menu: Contemporary takes on Portuguese classics. Be sure to sample the signature dish, Bacalhau à brás. The interior exudes an air of elegance and warmth. Step outside to a tranquil terrace drenched in sunlight, boasting a vibrant ambiance and providing welcome respite in the summer months.

→Largo Picadeiro 10 a 12, 1200-330
→21 346 0501

T O U C H

Loja das Conservas

You never thought canned food could be so fun—and so beautiful. This place has every Portuguese delicacy you could imagine in stylish containers, meaning great gifts or a fine snack on the go. Don't miss the mackerel fillet with spicy pickles and sardine eggs in olive oil.

→Rua do Arsenal 130, 1100-040
→911 181 210

A Vida Portuguesa

This specialty store stocks products that have been around for decades, with their original retro design and brand image preserved - we're talking furniture, shoes, wine, pans, porcelain, soap and even bathtubs. It's not a museum but could easily be one. This Intendente branch is the flagship but there are other satellites around the city.

→R. Anchieta 11, 1200-023
→21 346 5073

Vista Alegre

Vista Alegre, founded in 1824, is a notable porcelain brand in Portugal, and synonymous with beauty and quality. The shop in Lisbon is a haven for those who appreciate fine ceramics, crystal, glass, dinner sets and home decor.

→Largo do Chiado 20 23, 1200-108
→21 346 1401

Cortiço & Netos

Joaquim José Cortiço was a well-known expert on buying and selling discontinued lines of the traditional tiles used to embellish Lisbon's buildings. After he died, his grandchildren found an enormous collection of tiles in more than 900 different patterns and styles. To keep their grandfather's memory alive, they opened the store.

→R. Maria Andrade 37D, 1170-215
→21 136 2376

under the cover

This colourful magazine boutique stocks an international selection of niche publications, spanning an array of topics from record collection to food, literature, travel and art. A mandatory stop for any fan of paper and the things printed on it.

→R. Marquês Sá da Bandeira 88B, 1050-060
→915 374 707

S M E L L

Casa Independente

Resident band Fogo-Fogo play Cape Verdean music, which gives you an idea of the range of cultural influences at this lounge-cum-bar-cum-club, set up by two visionary women. Come during the day for the comfy vibe and nice garden, or at night for some serious tunes.

→Largo do Intendente Pina Manique 45, 1100-285

Lounge

A solid micro club for drinks to start or to end your night or to wind down. Every now and then you'll catch a band here, failing that there's always a DJ providing a solid groove.

→R. Moeda 1, 1200-275
→21 403 2712

LuxFrágil

The pinnacle of Lisbon's nightclubs, this venue boasts three floors that continue to distinguish themselves with top-tier bookings, inventive interior design, and breathtaking views overlooking the Tagus River. Anticipate waiting in line on weekends to gain entry to this nocturnal haven.

→Av. Infante D. Henrique a Sta Apolónia Cais da Pedra, Armazém A, 1950-376
→21 882 0890

Pavilhão Chinês

All five bar rooms here are packed with fascinating bric-à-brac, collected over the course of 70 years by the late owner. Order a drink from the smart barmen, play a round of pool and absorb the atmosphere.

→R. Dom Pedro V 89, 1250-093
→21 342 4729

Arroz Estúdios

The independent cultural center hosts a diverse array of events. The club nights range from Dubstep to straight techno – usually drawing a lively crowd on the dance floor. It's also worth checking out other events, such as outdoor cinema screenings or Live Jams.

→Avenida Infante Dom Henrique, AAFC, 1900-320

H E A R

F I L M

Lisbon Story, Wim Wenders, 1994

A sound engineer travels to Lisbon at the request of a friend, but finds him missing upon arrival. As he immerses himself in the city's rich soundscape, he starts to unravel a tale of love, loss, and longing amidst Lisbon's enchanting landscape.

LONDON

“I wander thro’ each charter’d street,
Near where the charter’d Thames does flow.
And mark in every face I meet
Marks of weakness, marks of woe.

In every cry of every Man,
In every Infants cry of fear,
In every voice: in every ban,
The mind-forg’d manacles I hear

How the Chimney-sweepers cry
Every blackning Church appalls,
And the hapless Soldiers sigh
Runs in blood down Palace walls

But most thro’ midnight streets I hear
How the youthful Harlots curse
Blasts the new-born Infants tear
And blights with plagues the Marriage hearse.”

William Blake

S E E

Greenwich Park

The park, with 74.5 hectares one of London's largest green spaces, offers spectacular views of the city and the River Thames. It's a serene spot to enjoy a picnic or explore the Royal Observatory.

→SE10 8QY
→0300 061 2380

Barbican Estate Office

A remarkable example of brutalist architecture, the design created by Chamberlin, Powell and Bon has consistently sparked controversy. The building is a combination of residential living and arts center. The Concert Hall serves as the home for the London Symphony Orchestra and the BBC Symphony Orchestra.

→City of London, Barbican EC2Y 8BY
→020 7029 3958

BAPS Shri Swaminarayan Mandir

The masterpiece of traditional temple design has been characterized as the United Kingdom's inaugural true Hindu temple. The mandir's lower level comprises a permanent exhibition area. Around it, you find a garden adorned with meticulously crafted flowerbeds, vibrant lawns, and skillfully shaped topiaries.

→Pramukh Swami Rd, Neasden NW10 8HW
→020 8965 2651

Two Temple Place

Also referred to as Astor House, this Neo-Gothic structure is renowned for its architectural style and houses significant artworks by artists such as Sir George Frampton RA, Nathaniel Hitch, and Thomas Nicholls.

→2 Temple Pl, Temple WC2R 3BD
→020 7836 3715

The Viktor Wynd Museum of Curiosities

Once a call center, the location curated by Viktor Wynd for The Last Tuesday Society melds museum and bar. The collection features traditional oddities like hairballs, two-headed lambs, and Fiji mermaids. The art collection spans centuries, including the most extensive display of Austin Osman Spare's work.

→11 Mare St, Cambridge Heath Rd E8 4RP
→020 8533 5297

T A S T E

St. JOHN Restaurant

Originally conceived as a simple bakery, this offshoot of the renowned St. John restaurant quickly expanded into the fully-fledged operation it now is. The menu focuses on simple, yet revisited classic English dishes with a less formal approach than its big sister. Here, there are no main courses but smaller, starter-sized dishes patrons are encouraged to share.

→26 St John St, Barbican EC1M 4AY
→020 7251 0848

Lyle's

This is what happened when the former head chef of St John Bread & Wine, James Lowe, opened his own restaurant in Shoreditch. Lyle's has clear influences from St. John, with the cuisine a celebration of revisited classics. Whether you go for the old favourites or the newcomers - be sure to expect a real British treat. Located in the Tea Building in the heart of hip.

→Tea Building, 56 Shoreditch High St E1 6GY
→020 3011 5911

Dishoom Carnaby

Dishoom, since its opening in Covent Garden in 2010, has revolutionized the perception of Indian restaurants in London with its homestyle cooking, retro ambiance, and exceptional cocktails. Despite its perpetual busy atmosphere, the restaurant, now boasting multiple locations, consistently attracts both locals and tourists with its authentic Indian starters and staples like lamb chops and chicken ruby, maintaining a consistently high standard across its menu.

→22 Kingly St, Carnaby W1B 5QP
→020 7420 9322

Brigadiers

A chic fusion of 1970s sports bar aesthetics and Indian Club Culture's art deco design, Brigadiers offers a unique culinary experience: The menu centers on a range of Indian barbecue techniques, utilizing tandoors, charcoal grills, rotisseries, wood ovens, and classic Indian smokers. The drink selection harmoniously complements the lively ambiance, providing beer, whiskey, and tap cocktails. Naturally, the establishment frequently screens sports events.

→1-5 Bloomberg Arcade EC4N 8AR
→020 3319 8140

Omotesando Koffee

Originally from Tokyo, Omotesando has found a home in London, serving Japanese-style coffee in a minimalist setting. The arrangement resembles a laboratory, complete with staff donning lab coats and a variety of flasks employed in coffee preparation. The open coffee station allows you to observe each stage of your drink's creation by their skilled baristas.

→8 Newman St W1T 1FB

Blanchette

The bistro presents a menu of straightforward, traditional, and innovative French dishes. The concept centers around the notion of communal dining. A well-curated collection of French wines stands ready to complement the culinary offerings.

→9 D'Arblay St W1F 8DR
→020 7439 8100

Normah's

Tucked within Queensway Market, this quaint, family-operated eatery offers superb Malaysian homestyle cuisine. Savour authentic favourites like Asam Pedas Seabass, King Prawn Laksa, and Nasi Lemak Beef Rendang. Secure a table by arriving early; seating is limited.

→23, 25 Queensway W2 4QJ
→07771 630828

Bubala Soho

The Soho outpost marks the second chapter for this thriving venture, evolving from its pop-up roots into a permanent success. It specializes in an entirely vegetarian Middle-Eastern fare. Dishes encompass labneh with confit garlic or zhoug and date syrup-coated fried aubergine. The approachable staff elucidates even the most unfamiliar ingredients, and they beautifully come to life on the plate.

→15 Poland St W1F 8QE

The Clove Club

A dining experience that combines creativity with a keen respect for ingredients, showcasing Britain's finest ingredients in an innovative menu: Think of Tart of sheep's milk yoghurt, wood-pigeon sausage with ketchup, lemonade and black pepper ice cream. It is a no-choice list of nine courses that are easy on the eyes and complex for the palate.

→Shoreditch Town Hall, 380 Old St EC1V 9LT
→020 7729 6496

Smoking Goat Shoreditch

In this lively and welcoming neighbourhood eatery, the culinary inspiration is deeply rooted in northern Thai cuisine. The menu showcases an array of small plates, with a standout being their celebrated barbecued Tamworth goat shoulder. Be sure to indulge in their distinctive cocktails like the Mango Negroni and the Blue Lychee Margarita.

→64 Shoreditch High St E1 6JJ

T O U C H

Beyond Retro Dalston

A huge vintage clothing store in East London: Boasting a diverse collection of over 12,000 unique pieces, from vintage sweatshirts to party dresses, there's a distinct find for every individual. The store is a hub for frequent pop-ups, workshops, and events, making it a recurring focal point for cultural and fashion-driven activities within the local community.

→92-100 Stoke Newington Rd N16 7XB
→020 7729 9001

magCulture

Magazine lovers worldwide follow Jeremy Leslie's magCulture website, without question the best source for news, interviews and debate about periodical publishing. Since late 2015, magCulture has been a shop too, housed appropriately in an old newsagent, on the route from Clerkenwell to Angel. The vigorous good health of small press publishers is clear to see in the variety – and heft – of titles from across the globe.

→270 St John St EC1V 4PE
→020 3759 8022

Daunt Books Marylebone

Arguably London's most beautiful bookshop with an original Edwardian interior and long book-lined galleries. It's one of the very best too, with knowledgeable and helpful staff who demonstrate an unerring knack for displaying the wares.

→84 Marylebone High St W1U 4QW
→020 7224 2295

Dover Street Market

Even if you don't have a penny to spare, this concept store is still worth a visit. Soak up the huge selection of contemporary clothes, shoes and designer objects, or simply have a chat with the charismatic salespeople – it's also usually quite interesting scoping out the other clientele, too.

→18-22 Haymarket SW1Y 4DG
→020 7518 0680

The Conran Shop Marylebone

Once a stable on Marylebone High Street, the iconic shop now offers three floors of contemporary furnishings, iconic products or vintage pieces, all reflecting a design ethos that values functionality and aesthetic. The cherished Rooftop Garden extends from the top-floor apartment, boasting outdoor furniture, lighting, and accessories.

→55 Marylebone High St W1U 5HS
→020 7723 2223

S M E L L

FOLD

An artist-led and community-driven nightclub with a focus on electronic music, spanning from Acid House to Techno. With 24-hour-long parties across two floors and a roster of talented resident DJs, the venue is ideal for immersive underground dance nights.

→Gillian House, Stephenson St E16 4SA

Rough Trade East

Since 1976, this name has served as an authority on the independent music scene. If your collection needs an update, pop in and ask which albums and artists the staff are currently backing. They know what they're talking about. While you're at it, grab a coffee or a bite to eat. The flagship store just off Brick Lane is also known for legendary live performances.

→Old Truman Brewery 91, Brick Ln E1 6QL
→020 7392 7788

Phonox

This club boasts a blend of top-tier DJs and an impressive setting featuring a Funktion One soundsystem. Keep an eye on the schedule for appearances by UK legends like Goldie and Grooverider, who occasionally grace the decks. Notably, the strict no-phones policy on the dance floor adds to the experience.

→418 Brixton Rd SW9 7AY
→020 7095 9411

Vortex

Despite its 30-year history as a jazz club, the venue maintains a consistently fresh and varied lineup of performers. For a glimpse of emerging talents, don't miss the Jam Sessions on Sunday evenings. Hosted by drummer Jas Kayser, pianist Rick Simpson, and tenor saxophonists Helena Kay and Riley Stone-Lonergan, these sessions promise an exciting musical experience.

→11 Gillett Square N16 8AZ
→020 7254 4097

Three Sheets

Renowned for its innovative libations, this modern local cocktail bar boasts a minimalist ambiance that directs attention to the drink craftsmanship. Under the guidance of "Drinks Development Queen" Rosey Mitchell, the menu undergoes weekly transformations, ensuring a dynamic experience for patrons.

→510b Kingsland Rd E8 4AB
→07718 648771

H E A R

F I L M

Lock Stock and Two Smoking Barrels, Guy Ritchie, 1998

In this iconic British crime comedy, four friends find themselves heavily in debt after a rigged card game. Their efforts to repay the debt pull them into London's underworld, leading to a series of comedic and thrilling events.

MADRID

"Madrid is a stranger's paradise, a home for everyone."

Antonio Machado

S E E

Temple of Debod

An ancient Egyptian temple in Spain. In 1972, Madrid's Parque del Oeste welcomed the reconstructed temple. However, the order of the gateways was altered during the restoration process, deviating from their original arrangement.

→C. de Ferraz, 1, 28008
→913 66 74 15

Antón Martín Market

At this bustling market, tradition and innovation dance a flavorful tango; The scene at the traditional stalls primarily features seasoned regulars going about their weekly routines. Meanwhile, at the restaurants, one can spot young couples pushing strollers here.

→C. de Sta. Isabel, 5, 28012
→913 69 06 20

Fountain of the Fallen Angel

A statue of Lucifer in the heart of Catholic territory? Yes, the Fallen Angel Fountain can be found in Madrid's Retiro Park. The piece is a creation of Ricardo Bellver (for the main sculpture) and Francisco Jareño (for the pedestal).

→Parque del Retiro, Glorieta del Ángel Caído, s/n, 28014

Museo ABC

Within the graceful walls of a converted brewery, you'll discover an homage to illustration, graphic design, and animation, inviting an exploration of modern Spanish culture through the lens of creativity.

→C. de Amaniel, 29, 28015

Torres Blancas

A testament to Madrid's architectural evolution in the late 1960s: The residential complex by Francisco Javier Sáenz de Oíza encompasses independent housing units while offering the conveniences of a tight-knit community. It blends the principles of Le Corbusier's unités d'habitation with the idea behind Frank Lloyd Wright's towers.

→Av. de América, 37, 28002
→691 50 21 29

T A S T E

La Venencia

Time seems to stand still in this traditional sherry bar, where the patina of the past is tangible in every dust-covered bottle and old-school tapas charm.

→Calle de Echegaray, 7, 28014
→914 29 73 13

ARAIA

This place aims to resurrect the spirit of a sunken island, bringing it back to life, a place nestled in the heart of the Mediterranean Sea, serving as a bridge between East and West, celebrating diversity in taste and style. So, expect Mediterranean delights and a masterfully crafted interior.

→C/ de Murillo, 3, 28010
→663 75 83 28

Estimar Madrid

For five generations, the Gotanegra family's life has been dedicated to serving the finest fish and seafood, initially in Barcelona. Today, Anna Gotanegra and Chef Rafa Zafra are the masterminds behind these artful creations, now also available at their second branch in Madrid.

→C. del Marqués de Cubas, 18, 28014
→914 29 20 52

Sacha Restaurant

A culinary icon presented in the charming guise of a cozy bistro. Tucked within an intimate dining setting adorned with monochromatic prints, humble wooden chairs, and pristine white tablecloths, Sacha Hormaechea orchestrates a menu of enduring classics, reimagined with a contemporary flair.

→Zona ajardinada, C. de Juan Hurtado de Mendoza, 11, Posterior, 28036
→913 45 59 52

Bar Santurce

A basic and authentic restaurant: Don Raul serves good food, and that's as simple as it gets. Try roasted sardines with Padrón peppers and a perfectly cooked squid. If you like yours with lemon – it's not provided by intention – bring your own as the regulars do.

→Plaza del Gral. Vara de Rey, 14, 28005
→646 23 83 03

Chocolatería San Ginés

Late-night craving for chocolate? Since 1894, this chocolatería has been dishing out irresistible Churros con chocolate. On the weekends, they're open 24 hours to satisfy your late-night cocoa hankerings.

→Pasadizo de San Ginés, 5, 28013
→913 65 65 46

Restaurante Casa Salvador

Pictures on the wall narrate the history of this establishment, which was originally founded as a tavern for bullfighters. Even today, the family-run restaurant exudes the cozy ambiance of a visit to your Spanish grandmother's house. The food aligns perfectly with this sentiment – traditional and homemade.

→C. de Barbieri, 12, 28004
→915 21 45 24

ACID Café

Immerse yourself in Japanese coffee culture within a serene minimalist setting. Here, the in-house bakery masterfully crafts sweet temptations infused with flavours from across the globe, including our exquisite Cannoli Siciliani – dipped in Ecuadorian chocolate and filled with homemade ricotta, pistachio, and fragrant rose petals.

→C. de la Verónica, 9, 28014

Verdejo Restaurante y Tabanco

The concept remained unchanged after the recent move to a new location. Marian Reguera's kitchen continues to emphasize the importance of showcasing high-quality ingredients, primarily sourced from small producers. While her culinary approach remains rooted in tradition, it is executed with the utmost finesse.

→Calle del General Díaz Porlier, 59, 28006
→910 11 22 48

Comparte Bistró

The small establishment, opened in 2022, offers a refined and creative cuisine with a French influence meant for sharing. The proprietors are a French-Andalusian couple, and their distinctive signature dishes include the unique steak tartare and tuna cheeks.

→C. de Belén, 6, 28004
→910 33 87 07

TOUCH

Ekseption

At two shops, fashion and avant-garde design seamlessly blend in a carefully curated collection of international pieces, ranging from Alaïa to Yukari Hirotani. Eduardo Samso is responsible for the interior design. Home textiles, cosmetics, and a selection of magazines complement the luxurious concept store offerings.

→C. de Velázquez, 28, 28001
→ 915 77 43 53

Mercado de Vallehermoso

Take a culinary journey: Local vegetable stalls, butchers, fishmongers, and poultry vendors not only supply the essentials for residents' pantries and fridges but also serve as the lifeblood for nearby bars and cozy, compact restaurants—some as small as a window.

→C. de Vallehermoso, 36, 28015
→914 47 54 67

Formaje

With a reverence for the art of cheese, the shop presents an impressive curation of Spanish and international selections, accompanied by artisanal bread and a fine selection of wines.

→Plaza de Chamberí, 9, local 3, 28010
→919 20 90 73

El Rastro / Fray Ceferino González

Every Sunday, a historic neighbourhood transforms into an eclectic outdoor bazaar, a haven for vintage and antique lovers, brimming with curiosity-sparking treasures.

→C. de Fray Ceferino González, 6, 28005
→900 818 070

WOW Concept

Hosted in the iconic former Hotel Roma building, this store offers an intriguing mix: gaming consoles stand side by side with luxury fashion. The stunning design spans three floors, and don't miss the chance to explore the tech garage in the basement.

→C.Gran Vía, 18, 28013
→917 51 78 31

S M E L L

Specia Atelier Bar

Skilled mixologists crafting artisan cocktails with precision: The spicy drinks are particularly sought-after favourites. If that's not to your taste, a myriad of milder concoctions awaits, featuring ingredients such as Madagascan vanilla, Colombian coffee, and toasted almonds.

→C. de las Infantas, 17, 28004
→666 37 77 16

Lula Club

A medium-sized concert hall primarily showcasing Spanish acts. Within the complex, there's also a club hosting various themed nights. International DJs like 2manyDJs also feature on the lineup.

→C.Gran Vía, 54, 28013
→917 37 80 40

CHA CHÁ

The narcissistic temple of nightlife in all its facets. Controversial door and sound policies, so it's best to check what's on the program. On the plus side: an open-minded crowd, unisex restrooms, and when the party gets going, there's no stopping it.

→C. de Alcalá, 20, 28014

Club Malasaña

A hybrid of a microclub and bar in the trendy neighbourhood of Malasaña. Alongside cocktails, they serve up a musical blend of House and Techno. Legendary are the Afrobeat parties on Sundays.

→C. de San Vicente Ferrer, 23, 28004
→689 20 00 04

Salmon Guru

Regularly featured on the list of the world's top 50 bars, this establishment serves up funky cocktails in a retro comic-themed ambiance adorned with vibrant neon accents. If the celestial alignment permits, after 11 pm, the music amplifies, and the atmosphere transforms into a lively party.

→Calle de Echegaray, 21, 28014
→910 00 61 85

HEAR

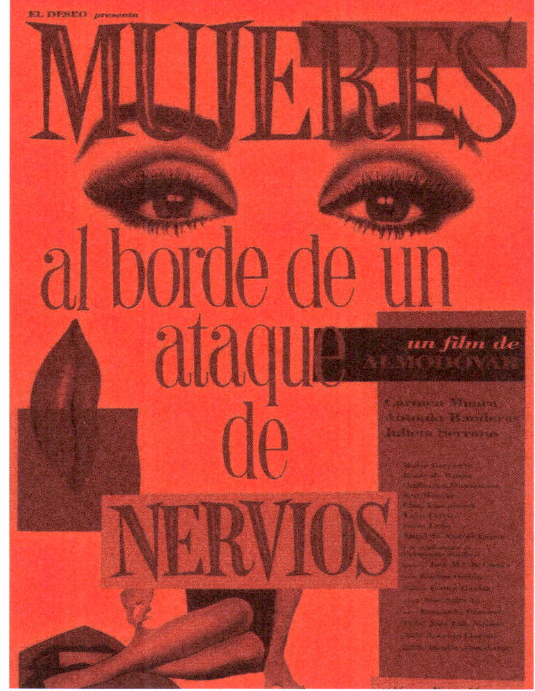

FILM

Women on the Verge of a Nervous Breakdown,
Pedro Almodóvar, 1988

Set in Madrid, this vibrant comedy follows the story of Pepa as she grapples with love, loss, and a series of outlandish events over 48 hours. Laden with humour, passion, and Almodóvar's signature style, it offers a delightful exploration of female resilience and solidarity amidst chaos.

MARSEILLE

“I am working with the enthusiasm of a man from Marseilles eating bouillabaisse, which shouldn’t come as a surprise to you because I am busy painting huge sunflowers.”

Vincent Van Gogh

S E E

Unité d'Habitation

The Unité d'habitation, or Housing Unit, is a groundbreaking architectural concept by Le Corbusier and Nadir Afonso. This modernist design influenced numerous housing developments across Europe. The most renowned is in Marseille, a testament to avant-garde design and urban planning.

→280 Bd Michelet, 13008

Massif des Calanques

The Calanques of Marseille offer rugged beauty and tranquillity within reach of the city. This natural area of dramatic cliffs and turquoise waters is an adventurer's delight.

→Massif des Calanques, 13009

Côte Bleue

Cote Bleue, near Marseille, is a stretch of coastline boasting clear waters and picturesque villages. It offers a peaceful counterpoint to the bustling city, with hiking trails and diving opportunities.

Friche la Belle de Mai

A former cigarette factory-turned-cultural center, this sprawling space takes mixed-use to a whole new level. Think skate park, indie radio station, locavore restaurant, art galleries, and artists' atelier. Plus hundreds of events to keep your social calendar packed.

→41 Rue Jobin, 13003
→04 95 04 95 95

Le Panier

The Panier district is the oldest neighbourhood. Renowned for its narrow, winding streets, vibrant street art, and unique boutiques, the district presents a charming, open-air museum atmosphere. La Vieille Charité is a must-see there.

→Le Panier, 13002

T A S T E

Chez Etienne

If pizza is the city's religion, this Sicilian institution is where it's most fervently worshipped. The wood-fired pizzas are simply topped with anchovies or cheese, an oozy mix of emmental and mozzarella. Now run by Etienne's grandson with as much gusto as his late Nonno.

→43 Rue Lorette, 13002
→06 16 39 78 73

La Cantinetta

Here lies one of the city's best garden patios, hidden from the hubbub of Cours Julien. An Italian bistro beloved for its linguini alla vongole and housemade pasta by Luigi, a Neapolitan transplant. Burrata, antipasti, and panettone pain perdu, aka Italian French Toast, round out the menu. At night, they have two services--book the latter if you want to linger.

→24 Cr Julien, 13006
→04 91 48 10 48

Toinou les Fruits de Mer

One of the city center's last écaillers, this family-run institution has been slinging seafood and fish since 1956. Depending on the season, the catch can include Côte Bleue sea urchins, Bouzigues oysters, tellines, and sea bass. Dine inside, on the terrace, or order a platter to bring to a dinner party or the beach.

→58 Av. Henri Malacrida, 13100 Aix-en-Provence, France
→04 42 58 08 59

Figure | Cave à manger

Behind its unassuming facade, you will be welcomed by tantalizing tapas plates alongside an array of splendid nectars. An evening's highlights might include playful Dauphine potatoes accompanied by apricot condiment and herb mayo, marinated peppers lounging over smoky mezcal stracciatella with juicy peaches and hazelnuts.

→90 Bd Vauban, 13006
→04 65 57 08 87

Tuba Club - Cabanons et Restaurant

Perched on a rock overlooking the sea, the restaurant at the Tuba Hotel boasts a terrace with an astounding ocean view. This former diving club has been transformed into a dining delight. Recent delicacies included a fresh tarama, a sharp bream carpaccio with olives and eggplant caviar, and a massive Greek salad to share.

→2 Bd Alexandre Delabre, 13008
→04 91 25 13 16

Grand Bar des Goudes

This establishment's history dates back to 1920, today, it's a beloved local institution, helmed by Didier Tani, who started working there at age 14 under his father's ownership. The current chef Christophe Thullier is committed to freshness and quality, personally selecting fish right off the boats every morning.

→28 Rue Désiré Pelaprat, 13008
→04 91 73 43 69

Atelier Renata

Behind the green door of Atelier Renata, named after the owner Erika Blu's grandmother, one could anticipate an exquisite Italian dinner. Erika, a self-taught chef from Rome and Venice, now delivers her sentimental food in this former artist's studio, transformed into a dining room with Persian rugs, family photos, and two pianos.

→2 Rue Guy Fabre, 13001
→09 79 02 97 15

Ourea

Chef Mathieu Roche is on a first-name basis with farmers and his dishes sprout seasonal produce alongside local lamb and freshly caught fish. The pretty plating pairs well with the pops of colour in the intimate 32-seat bistro he owns with his partner, Camille. Dinner is a 4-course set menu while lunch alongside lawyers from the nearby Palais de Justice is a la carte.

→72 Rue de la Paix Marcel Paul, 13006
→04 91 73 21 53

Petrin Couchette

A café-bakery that beckons you to settle in with its wooden facade, beamed ceilings, and yellow-tiled counter. Led by Basile Milou and his exceptional team, they offer extraordinary sourdough breads and sandwiches featuring ancient grains. Sweet tooths can enjoy glazed lemon cake or a robust chocolate brownie before continuing on their journey with a loaf of spelt bread or a delicious sandwich in hand.

→7 Cr Saint-Louis, 13001
→04 91 39 00 21

Taste 91

David Mijoba has cooked up a novel concept in the former premises of Venus, located in the heights of Vauban, offering exciting cuisine and a wine cellar in a cave! His menu offers an impressive array of vegetarian and seafood dishes, such as fresh Mediterranean anchovies marinated in Phu Quoc pepper, accompanied by salt-crusted beetroot and succulent Gascon black pork belly croutons.

→79 Bd Vauban, 13006
→04 91 92 03 53

T O U C H

Maison Empereur

France’s oldest hardware store is one of the world’s best places to shop. Ask a clerk in a blue jacket to help you sift through the staggering 50,000 items, including Opinel knives, Le Serail soap, and old-timey toys. Lovers of heritage wear, head to the clothing store next door for Camargue cowboy shirts and Breton wool sweaters.

→4 Rue des Récolettes, 13001
→04 91 54 02 29

Epicerie L’IDEAL

Food journalist Julia Sammut stocks the shelves of this grocery store/café with finds from her travels. At lunchtime, the communal tables fill up fast for Mediterranean-inspired fare. The friendly staff are like family, hence the cat behind the cash register. Friday night apéro spills into the weekends.

→11 Rue d'Aubagne, 13001
→09 80 39 99 41

Maison Blaize

Steeped in over two centuries of history, this salon du thé showcases the healing tisanes of the herbalist Pére Blaize. Among the 12 signature teas, try the minty Notre Dame de la Garde or the anise Chateau d'If. Sip the teas here or take them to go, along with essential oils, herbs, and other plant-based remedies.

→5 Rue Meolan et du Père Blaize, 13001
→04 91 73 10 56

Jogging store

This former butcher shop now serves the city's most cutting-edge fashion like trend-setting pieces from le Sud's Jacquemus to Moscow's Walk of Shame. While this concept store oozes cool, the vibe is unpretentiously Mediterranean, like the track pants (le jogging) sported by many Marseillais. In the summer, the hidden garden and outdoor kitchen out back blossom into a bistro for talented chefs.

→103 Rue Paradis, 13006
→04 91 81 44 94

Marché aux Poissons

The fish market stands as the most renowned of Marseille's markets. It originated in 1909 within the old port and has remained there ever since. Operating every morning throughout the year, it is advisable to arrive early to secure the fish of your choice.

→2 Quai du Port, 13002

S M E L L

Bar des Amis

Near the city's best surf spot, this beachside bar de quartier is all about good vibes. Mojitos and spritzes at happy hour, DJs spinning funk into the wee hours, epic sunset views, and a friendly staff and a stellar pan de bagnat, thanks to owner Ivan's niçois roots. Along with his partner, Mélanie, the former clients have infused new energy into BDA and returned it to its heyday.

→23 Av. de la Pointe Rouge, 13008
→04 91 96 17 62

Bar de la Marine

There's both disappointment and joy associated with the renowned Bar de la Marine, brought to life by Marcel Pagnol and featured in his famous trilogy. Disappointment, as depicted in the interior scenes of the films, was not actually in Marseille's Old Port, but shot in a studio in Paris. However, joyfully, there is now a new Bar de la Marine, established in the vicinity of the original bar with a stunning view of the Old Port.

→15 Quai de Rive Neuve, 13007
→04 91 54 95 42

Bar Gaspard

A cocktail boite infused with a tiki vibe. Fishnet lamps hang above the fish tank bar that's topped in Mediterranean blue. Dive into the small menu of expertly shaken drinks. Check social media for the popular chef collaborations the owner, Ben, organizes.

→7 Boulevard Notre Dame, 13006
→06 88 23 86 66

Baby Club

Hedonistic micro-club with a musical spectrum that spans between techno and house, featuring local residents and French bookings. Typically, it hosts a lively and dancing crowd ranging from 20 to mid-30 years old, often reaching maximum capacity.

→2 Rue André Poggioli, 13006
→06 19 98 29 22

Danceteria

The last bastion of late-night indie clubs in the city center. The venue is not large, and the audience mixes well during the second half of the night. Musically, electro and techno are on the program, but also related exotica.

→18 Rue Saint-Saëns, 13001

H E A R

F I L M

Fanny, Marc Allégret, 1932

A part of Marcel Pagnol's Marseille Trilogy, this romantic drama portrays the story of Fanny, torn between her love for a barkeep and responsibility towards her child. The movie presents a vivid picture of life in the port city of Marseille during the 1930s.

MILAN

“One once wandered through desolate suburbs and roamed along railways, fascinated by the picturesque romanticism of Porta Ticinese and its channels. Now it is a metropolis of skyscrapers, slightly futuristic and slightly provincial: a mix between risotto and steel—which amuses me.”

Alberto Lattuada

S E E

Gallaratese II Housing

Designed by Carlo Aymonino and Aldo Rossi during the late 1960s, this complex is occasionally nicknamed the “Red Dinosaur.” This moniker alludes to both the distinctive reddish hue of the buildings and the uniqueness of of their Brutalist architecture.

→Via Enrico Falck, 53, 20151
→02 353 9907

Villa Reale

A splendid Neoclassical palace, complete with a picturesque English-style garden featuring an artificial lake designed by Leopoldo Pollack. This enchanting setting beckons visitors to take leisurely strolls amidst its scenic splendour. Adjacent to the villa stands the Padiglione

d’Arte Contemporanea, a dedicated exhibition space showcasing contemporary art.

→Via Palestro, 16, 20121
→02 8844 5943

Via Abramo Lincoln

A small pocket of colour just north of Piazza Cinque Giornate. The street, likely not widely known, exudes genuine charm with its two-story pastel-toned villas, vibrant shutters, and floral embellishments on the gates.

→Via Abramo Lincoln, 20129

Achille Castiglioni Foundation

The foundation is home to a museum that pays homage to one of Italy’s most influential designers. Housed within the designer’s former studio, this museum serves as a testament

to the remarkable legacy of Castiglioni's work and the profound influence of Italian design on a global scale. Visits to the museum are available by appointment.

→Piazza Castello, 27, 20121
→02 805 3606

Università Bocconi

The complex is home to one of Europe's leading business schools, and offers a glimpse into Milan's academic life. The site's new construction is part of a broader, state-of-the-art growth project, with a focus on ecological sustainability. The impressive architecture is the work of the Japanese star architects Kazuyo Sejima and Ryue Nishizawa from the SANAA studio.

→Via Roberto Sarfatti, 25, 20100
→02 403434

T A S T E

Erba Brusca

Alice and Luca elevate the concept of farm-to-table dining to a whole new level. Their restaurant is conveniently situated just 50 meters around the corner from an expansive vegetable garden spanning approximately 4,000 square meters. This garden serves as the source for their ever-evolving menu, which is tied to the daily harvest.

→Alzaia Naviglio Pavese, 286, 20142
→351 516 6021

Quartiere Stadera

Food like that of a nonna from Campagna, who knows both the past and the present. Aldo Ritrovato's cuisine is loved by many. The small, narrow restaurant with seating around the open kitchen can get quite crowded, especially in the winter.

→Quartiere Stadera, 20141

Osteria Conchetta

A reliable traditional Italian neighbourhood trattoria, away from the tourist crowds, offering a warm and classical ambiance. The menu pays homage to the simplicity and refinement of Lombardy cuisine. Be sure to sample the Vodka Risotto with Grana Padano or the Orecchia D'elefante.

→Via Conchetta, 8, 20136
→02 837 2917

Il Salumaio di Montenapoleone - since 1957

An institution renowned for its fine Italian delicacies served in an elegant setting. During the summer months, the courtyard is the perfect spot to savour your meal. It's worth noting that the service can occasionally be a bit brusque.

→Via Santo Spirito, 10, 20121
→02 7600 1123

Lon Fon

Tired of spaghetti al pomodoro? Milan's Chinatown offers noodles with different flavours – for example, Cantonese. The dumplings from the Tsui family are worth the culinary sidestep.

→Via Lazzaretto, 10, 20124
→02 2940 5153

Remulass

Orange and blue are the colours of the small restaurant, tastefully adorned with mid-century reminiscences. Just as fresh as the ambiance, there's a contemporary twist in the kitchen. Italian dishes are given a modern interpretation, occasionally with an Asian influence.

→Via Nino Bixio, 21, 20129
→02 5251 7356

Antica Gelateria Sartori

Andrea Sartori laid the foundation for the ice cream stand in the 1930s. Today, Andrea's grandson, Anthony, who shares the same passion for gelato, manages the business. The flavours remain classic, such as Malaga and Zabaione, in keeping with the company motto: Tradition above all else!

→Piazza Luigi di Savoia, 20125

Osteria Alla Concorrenza

A small osteria in Porta Venezia with simple wooden tables and friendly owners. The menu is displayed on a large board at the entrance. They offer simple Italian treats, including various types of focaccia, cold cuts, and cheese.

→Via Melzo, 12, 20129
→02 9167 2012

Torrefazione Moka Hodeidah

A cozy, tiny shop with its own roastery. They offer numerous, sometimes super-exclusive coffee varieties that you can enjoy on the spot or purchase as beans. It's also a great place for a quick breakfast.

→Via Piero della Francesca, 8, 20154
→02 342472

Frangente

Federico Sisti, the master of the open kitchen in this cozy eatery, showcases his skillful hand in preparing classic Italian cuisine with a contemporary twist. One of his signature dishes is the Veal Sweetbreads

→Via Panfilo Castaldi, 4, 20124
→02 9684 4851

T O U C H

Wok Store

Federica Zambon and Simona Citarella founded a luxury concept store, featuring lesser-known brands like Heureu and Agolde, along with renowned designers like Proenza Schouler and Jil Sander. Be sure to explore their on-site events as well.

→Viale Col di Lana, 5a, 20136
→351 163 6423

Commerce

This is not just one of the finest independent bookstores in town but also a must-visit venue for related events such as performances, exhibitions, and panels. Don't forget to explore their limited merchandise as well.

→Via Alessandro Tadino, 30, 20124

Terroir Milano

Founded by Gabriele Ornati in 2017, this food shop offers a meticulously curated selection of exquisite products sourced from artisans and local producers. They also feature a diverse range of biodynamic wines, primarily sourced from lesser-known, smaller winemakers.

→Via Macedonio Melloni, 33, 20129
→02 3824 6796

Frip Milano

A small fashion store, dedicated to cutting-edge fashion since the 1990s, with a strong emphasis on Scandinavian designers. They were the pioneers who introduced brands like ACNE and Henrik Vibskov to Milan.

→Corso di Porta Ticinese, 16, 20123
→02 832 1360

Corso Como, 10

The mythical concept store features a wonderful bookshop, an art gallery, a cafe, and the bespoke fashion department. In addition to the usual suspects of the high fashion scene, the offering includes numerous products that have emerged from collaborations between the shop and brands like Clarks, Castañer, or Zanellato.

→Corso Como, 10, 20154

S M E L L

Dude Club

Experience Milan's vibrant electronic music scene at this venue. It features a cutting-edge sound system and hosts an array of international DJs. Legends like Derrick May and Marcel Dettmann frequently perform here, all across two pulsating floors

→Via Carlo Boncompagni, 44, 20139

Plastic

Since the 1980s and after several renovations and relocations, the club has been a go-to spot for the 'see and be seen' crowd. The process starts right at the door, where those who make it inside are welcomed by a diverse array of nocturnal creatures of all ages.

→Via Gargano, 15, 20139

Bar Basso

Decades ago it became the first-ever Milanese joint to introduce the "Aperitif" to everyday people. It remains a not-to-be-missed meeting place, known primarily for its signature cocktail: the Negroni Sbagliato, invented here and served on ice in huge scenographic glasses. Warning: Do not ask for an “aperitivo”. Here you will drink cocktails at the counter with nuts, olives, and chips; the way it’s been done for years.

→Via Plinio, 39, 20133
→02 2940 0580

Apollo Milano

The Rollover crew, led by Marcellina and Tiberio, is renowned for their wild parties. Their specialty: transforming restaurants into clubs, just like here. In the fall of 2023, they embark on another season at Apollo with residents and guest DJs like Hunnee from Berlin.

→Via Giosuè Borsi, 9/2, 20143
→02 3826 0176

Mag Cafe

First, you have to find your way to the intimate MAG Café. Here, the gatekeepers will grant you access to the Prohibition-era speakeasy bar. What can you expect once you’ve made it inside? A true vintage atmosphere, fabulous cocktails, and occasional live piano music.

→Ripa di Porta Ticinese, 43, 20143
→02 3956 2875

H E A R

F I L M

Rocco and His Brothers, Luchino Visconti, 1960

This neorealist film showcases the plight of the Parondi family, who move from rural southern Italy to industrial Milan. As they grapple with poverty, family conflict, and modern city life, the film provides a deep, empathetic study of family dynamics and societal change.

MUNICH

“If you don’t like Munich, I don’t know which part of Germany you could like.”

Angela Merkel

S E E

Eisbach

Surfing in the middle of Munich: the Eisbach River is the largest city-centre location for river surfing, with a steady stream of waves emerging by the entrance of the English Garden. The waves can reach about half a metre and are only recommended for professional surfers.

→Eisbach, Munich, Germany

Olympiapark München

Even though the Olympic Games in Munich are forever associated with the terrible terrorist attack, the grounds today represent the architectural vision of the early 1970s: This is particularly evident in the design of the park and the iconic tent-like roof structure. During the summer months, visitors have the opportunity to ascend this

remarkable edifice as part of guided tours.

→Spiridon-Louis-Ring 21, 80809

Goetz Collection

The Herzog & de Meuron building houses the contemporary art collection of Ingvild Goetz, In order to understand the significance of her collection, you should be privy to the fact that Andy Warhol once created a portrait of Goetz. She collected art from names like Damien Hirst, Cy Twombly, Roni Horn and Cindy Sherman long before they became famous to a wider audience.

→Oberföhringer Str. 103, 81925
→089 95939690

Müller'sches Volksbad

One of Europe's most beautiful public indoor swimming pools. It was Munich's first indoor pool when it opened in 1901. Designed by architect Carl Hocheder, it was influenced by Oriental hammams and Roman thermal spas, focusing on decorative Baroque details that will transform your aquatic exercise jaunt into a real visual experience.

→Rosenheimer Str. 1, 81667
→089 23615050

Viktualienmarkt

One of the most famous German food markets: a bustling open-air market featuring stalls selling fresh produce, gourmet foods, and local delicacies. It's also a great place for breakfast and lunch, offering a sensory feast that reflects Bavaria's culinary diversity.

→Viktualienmarkt

T A S T E

Brothers Restaurant

Chef Daniel Bodamer represents a product-centred modern cuisine with a classic foundation. This approach earned the young restaurant a Michelin star within just a few months. Nevertheless, the owners aim to maintain a relaxed and unpretentious atmosphere in the small, straightforwardly designed establishment.

→Kurfürstenstraße 31, 80801
→089 45461930

Ornella Bar & Restaurant

Golden mirrors and stucco on the pillars, inviting furniture – in the restaurant opened in 2022, comfort takes precedence. The same applies to the cuisine of Christian Wurmsam. He serves Italian and Japanese dishes here, not as a fusion, but separately and in high quality.

→Platzl 4, 80331
→089 26201560

Fraunhofer-Gesellschaft

The history of this neighbourhood tavern goes back to 1774, and some of the interior elements are more than 100 years old. On the menu are Bavarian classics like Schweinshaxn (pork knuckle) and Leberknödln (liver dumplings).

→Hansastraße 27c, 80686
→089 12050

Beim Sedlmayr

Opened in 1990 by the Bavarian actor Walter Sedlmayr, this place boasts a traditional tavern interior with simple wooden tables and wood panelling on the walls. The establishment offers a fixed menu featuring classic Bavarian delicacies as well as some offal dishes such as veal sweetbreads, veal heart, or kidneys.

→Westenriederstraße 14, 80331
→089 226219

Bar Bravo

A laid-back Italian-style daytime joint, founded by nightlife veterans Marlon Schuler and Damir Stabek, it is all about simple and timeless design elements. It's adorned with classic wooden bistro chairs, marble surfaces, and mirrors. Here, you'll find the expected morning espresso, a variety of pasta options for lunch, and in the evenings, an aperitivo.

→Fraunhoferstraße 20, 80469
→089 81302715

Isar Alm

A lesser-known beer garden situated by the river, at the fringes of an allotment community. The owner holds a commendable philosophy: a commitment to using only organic ingredients, boasting an on-site microbrewery, and offering quality wine – a rarity in such a laid-back setting.

→Nithartstraße 8, 81541
→089 6518154

Wirtshaus Hohenwart

The place is renowned for crafting the city's finest Käsespätzle (Swabian cheese noodles), serving one of the city's best schnitzels, and offering a delightful Schweinsbraten (pig roast) complemented by fresh Augustiner beer. Additionally, they boast an open bowling alley, which you can easily sign up for.

→Gietlstraße 15, 81541
→089 69397575

Schumann's

The owner, Charles Schumann, is a legend, not only as a bartender but also as a fashion icon, even at his advanced age – this man embodies style. The same can be said for his bar at Hofgarten, which also offers classic food prepared just the way he likes it: a solid pasta, risotto, a well-cooked steak, or a fresh salad.

→Odeonspl. 6-7, 80539
→089 229060

Giorgia Trattoria

It doesn't get more colourful: The design of the trattoria is intended to evoke Milan in the 1980s – with ubiquitous floral patterns, marble tables, and a mirrored ceiling. The cuisine is straightforwardly Italian – from pizza to pasta – everything is 100% homemade, and ingredients are sourced from small producers in Italy.

→Weißenburger Str. 2, 81667

MiRA Café - Studio

A small place is created where art and good coffee blend together. The wake-up call comes from the Vits roastery, the espresso machine from Victoria Arduino is a beauty, and the cakes and quiches are homemade. In addition, there are changing exhibitions.

→Heimeranstraße 32, 80339

T O U C H

Holareidulijö

Bavarian traditional attire is legendary and a must at beer festivals like Oktoberfest. Michaela Kleinh's tiny shop is filled to the ceiling with vintage Bavarian clothing items. How about a pair of short trousers made from deer leather?

→Schellingstraße 81, 80799
→089 2717745

Sois Blessed

A classic concept store for adults: Curated fashion, interior pieces, especially noteworthy are the newly reupholstered furniture classics, the daytime gastronomy, and the flower shop that make the location a jack-of-all-trades. It's nice that the owners also devote themselves to numerous charity projects.

→Prannerstraße 10, 80333
→089 20941800

Hier-Store

The minimalist design and exposed walls ensure that the products take center stage, and in this small concept store, the offerings change regularly: fashion, accessories or cosmetics – everything is finely curated. The unique twist: all the manufacturers showcased here are from the region.

→Innere Wiener Straße 24, 81667
→089 23792039

Alva-Morgaine

Kimonos from Kyoto, porcelain tigers from Nigeria, or sparkling Glamrock boots from the 1970s – Alva Morgaine collects whatever catches her fancy. In her eponymous store, she can recount a story for each piece. For vintage fashion enthusiasts, this little shop is a treasure trove with unexpected depth.

→Hans-Sachs-Straße 9, 80469
→089 12253355

S M E L L

Milla

A cozy club with live gigs four to five nights a week. The lineup leans toward indie music, but the bookers have a knack for discovering wonderful, undiscovered bands from both the local and international scenes. It's always worth checking out their program from time to time.

→Holzstraße 28, 80469
→089 18923101

Goldener Reiter

A dark basement club with a rich history. Allegedly, Queen's Freddy Mercury and his entourage partied here in the 1980s. Nowadays, it attracts a younger, diverse crowd who come to groove to the house and techno beats spun by resident DJs.

→Theklastraße 1, 80469

The High

The small neighbourhood bar is situated in the trendy area between Gärtnerplatz and Viktualienmarkt. On weekends, it can get quite crowded. In addition to the eponymous "Highballs," Ella and André also serve classic cocktails to suit your taste.

→Blumenstraße 15, 80331

Blitz Club

The Techno flagship on the Isar River: The club is located in a former congress hall. During its renovation, the central focus was on optimizing the listening experience, to the extent that room geometry and materials were adapted accordingly. International luminaries like Jeff Mills and Luke Slater are regular guests.

→Access via Ludwigsbrücke, Museumsinsel 1, 80538
→089 380126561

Bar Gabányi

A classical bar with high-quality drinks and distinguished staff who occasionally engage to shape the evening's atmosphere in their own way. Open until 5 AM on weekends, with some light bites available as well. Even when DJs are spinning, the atmosphere remains intimate, and the music serves as background ambiance.

→Beethovenpl. 2, 80336
→089 51701805

H E A R

F I L M

Rote Sonne, Rudolf Thome, 1970

A cult film of the New German Cinema movement, it presents a group of young women who have made a pact to murder their lovers after three days of being together. Their casual approach towards violence and relationships adds a darkly comedic touch to this social satire.

NAPLES

"Naples was a crazy city – they were as crazy as me."

Diego Maradona

S E E

Lido Virgilio

This beach invites visitors to experience the stunning coastline around the city, just a 20-minute taxi ride away. Its sandy beaches and crystalline waters offer a taste of the city's beautiful Mediterranean environment. You can rent beach chairs and colourful sunshades on-site, and the beach shack takes care of your hunger and thirst.

→Via Lido Miliscola, 33, 80070
→081 523 2722

Pio Monte della Misericordia

The historic complex also includes a church famous for Caravaggio's painting "Sette opere di Misericordia" (The Seven Works of Mercy). The first floor hosts one of the city's important museums, the Quadreria del Pio Monte della

Misericordia, with its impressive collection of paintings from the 17th and 18th centuries.

→Via dei Tribunali, 253, 80139
→081 446944

Mercato della Pignasecca

The oldest market in the city is located in the alleys of the Spanish Quarter. This is also where the heart of the locals beats: fruits and vegetables, meat, offal, and fish are offered amidst Maradona and Napoli football shirts or flip-flops.

→Via Pignasecca, 28, 80134

The Torretta market

The covered market offers the convenience of one-stop shopping without a supermarket atmosphere. With a mix of

permanent stalls and shops, you'll discover a wealth of fresh ingredients: deli meats, cheeses, a variety of meats, seafood, a bakery, and the tucked-away shop Casa del Tortellino for fresh pasta.

→Via Ferdinando Galiani, 25-33, 80122

Lia Rumma

One of the pioneers of contemporary art in the city, this gallery was founded in 1971 and has since played a fundamental role in discovering new artistic trends such as Arte Povera, Minimal Art, Land Art, and Conceptual Art. Since 1999, Lia Rumma has also operated a branch in Milan.

→Via Vannella Gaetani, 12 1° piano / 1st floor, 80121
→081 1981 2354

T A S T E

Osteria Da Antonio

A classic trattoria with a strong focus on fish and seafood: Antonio's cozy restaurant features signature dishes like the Zuppa Frutti di Mare and Linguine al Profumo di Limone. The latter is a pasta dish made with linguine noodles tossed in a zesty lemon-flavoured sauce with razor clams.

→Via Agostino Depretis, 143, 80100
→081 551 0138

Mimi alla Ferrovia

Since 1944, a classic for Neapolitan cuisine: Today, the owner Salvatore himself is in the kitchen, who has also cooked in Kyoto and Tokyo, and adds some new accents, but all of them are based on traditional cuisine. This reads as follows: Tubettoni (pasta) but with yellow tomato sauce, Confit Datterini with green chillies and provola or red shrimp tartare with 'fake egg'.

→Via Alfonso D'Aragona, 19/21, 80139
→081 553 8525

Tripperia O'Russ Napoli

Not for the faint of heart: Tripe is as much a part of Neapolitan home cooking as tomatoes and olive oil. In this simple eatery, you'll find this specialty not only served very fresh but also in numerous different preparations: as a soup, as a salad, or with pasta.

→Via S. Eframo Vecchio, 68, 80137
→081 599 1701

Pintauro

A charming old-school bakery where the founder's portrait hangs in a golden frame above the marble counter, surrounded by religious icons. During peak hours, there's often a queue. It's also a great place to pick up a sweet pastry to enjoy with your espresso at the nearby bar.

→Via Toledo, 275, 80132
→348 778 1645

Gambrinus

This cafe is one of the most famous in the city – it is a piece of the city's history. Since 1860, in the ambiance of the Belle Époque, coffee and pastries have been served here. Founded as a literary cafe, personalities such as Oscar Wilde, Ernest Hemingway, and Jean-Paul Sartre found their way to the counter.

→Via Chiaia, 1, 80132
→081 417582

Europeo Mattozzi

An institution in Naples since 1852, it boasts a beautiful ambiance with white-covered tables. While pizza is a main highlight on the menu, the kitchen also serves up Italian classics like fried zucchini blossoms and fine pasta dishes of reliable quality.

→Via Marchese Campodisola, 4, 80133
→081 552 1323

Caffe Mexico

The classic cafe chain operates various locations in the city. What unites them all is the classic 1960s interior with plenty of steel and orange accents, the robust old La San Marco espresso machines, and skilled baristas brewing the roasted Arabica blend. In the summer, you can order a coffee frappé.

→Via Taddeo da Sessa, 77, 80143
→081 269642

Pizzaria la notizia 53

No Naples visit is complete without a real pizza. There are plenty of opportunities in the city for that. Enzo also operates three shops, but his Notizia 94 is our favourite because it presents exceptional flavours that continue to evolve the tradition.

→Via Michelangelo da Caravaggio, 53, 80126
→081 7142155

Aria

Naples can also offer fine dining experiences. If you're willing to spend some Liras, Chef Paolo Barrale is the perfect choice. In an elegant and intimate setting, he serves an inspiring cuisine that is rooted in Southern Italian tradition but deconstructed and reinterpreted in a novel way.

→Via Loggia dei Pisani, 2-14, 80133
→081 843 0195

'A Figlia d''o Marenaro

Near the Botanical Garden, you'll find this establishment that opened in 1955. On the menu, you'll find fish and seafood in an elegant atmosphere. Don't miss the exquisite Paccheri al Grancho (Paccheri with crab), but be sure to save room for the pistachio cheesecake at the end.

→Via Foria, 180/182, 80137
→081 440827

T O U C H

Rubinacci

In Italian fashion, there are regional differences, and Naples is known for its unique style. This iconic brand was founded by Gennaro Rubinacci in the 1930s and now has its own stores in Milan and London. At the flagship store, a true gentleman can have his suit tailored to perfection.

→Via Chiaia, 149, 80121
→081 415793

Cravatte sartoriali E. & G. Cappelli

You don’t wear a tie? Visit Patrizio Cappelli’s atelier and let yourself be convinced to give it a try. For over 30 years, he has been designing ties that offer an Italian interpretation of classic British styles. You can also get ties and pocket squares here customized to your own taste and measurements.

→Via Cavallerizza a Chiaia, 37, 80121
→08 140 0166

Grimaldi & C. Editori

The bookstore and the antiquarian shop are housed in an old chapel. Book enthusiasts can browse for hours in this small store. Don’t forget to ask the owners about their in-house editions as well.

→Via Carlo Poerio, 50-51, 80121
→08 140 6021

meria Rafele ‘O Lattaro

In the city, there are several opportunities to stock up on local food items. We love this little store not only for its selection of regional cheese and salami but also because you can enjoy small platters right on the spot.

→Via dei Tribunali, 40, 80138
→081 449169

M. Cilento & Fratello

A men’s fashion store that seems to have stepped out of a bygone era, founded in 1780. The products offered exude noble elegance and top-notch quality, including many in-house creations. The shoe section is particularly intriguing, as they also sell custom-made footwear.

→Riviera di Chiaia, 203/204, 80121
→081 551 3363

S M E L L

Basic Club

The techno and house flagship on the outskirts of the city. The bookings also contribute to the history of underground clubbing with many legends like Kenny Dope or Underground Resistance. They have a killer sound system that pays homage to the iconic 1970s club, The Loft, in NYC.

→Viale Giovanni Boccaccio, 9, 80040
→339 802 8991

NAPLES

La Fesseria

Bonsai Cocktailbar, where the young crowd gathers on weekends, often spilling onto the street. The cocktails, especially the house creations, surprise with new flavours. The cheerful staff is also happy to share tips on where the party continues afterward.

→Via Giovanni Paladino, 17, 80138
→081 1882 3409

Soul Express

A club collective that plays at different locations depending on the season. An Aperitivo DJ set in the park can easily turn into a wild party. International names are also part of the lineup, firing up house, disco, Italo, and Balearic tunes. Be sure to check their Instagram for updates.

→Via Ilioneo, 38, 80124
→340 820 3150

L'Antiquario

A classic speakeasy bar with an unassuming entrance and a doorbell. Inside, the best mixologists await to surprise guests with their creations. Be sure to try the house-made Negroni and Americano variations.

→Via Vannella Gaetani, 2, 80121
→081 764 5390

Duel Club

A techno club with an underground vibe. Housed in a former cinema, everyone dances on one floor to beats beyond 120 BPM. The bookings are excellent, with a mix of national acts and international heavyweights like Ellen Allien, Len Faki, or Jeff Mills.

→Via Antiniana, 80078

H E A R

F I L M

Hand of God, Paolo Sorrentino, 2021

This coming-of-age story, set in 1980s Naples, is a semi-autobiographical account of Sorrentino's own youth. It explores themes of love, loss, and the role of fate against the backdrop of a city where beauty and hardship coexist.

OSLO

“Oslo in the summertime; nobody can fall asleep, staring out the window from my bed. At 4 A.M., the sun is up. Look, the sky is peppered with sea birds and with crows all cackling.”

Of Montreal

S E E

Deichman Bjørvika

The Norwegian architectural firms Lund Hagem Arkitekter and Atelier Oslo designed the impressive main building of the country's largest library. Particularly intriguing inside is the Future Library, created by the artist Katie Paterson. This section houses texts that will only be published one hundred years after the construction of the library began.

→Anne-Cath, Vestlys plass 1, 0150
→23 43 29 00

Munch

The most famous Norwegian painter has been exhibited in his own museum since 1963. However, since 2021, it is housed in a spectacular 13-story new building designed by the architects from the Spanish firm Estudio Herreros. The

building, made of recycled concrete and recycled aluminum, is the largest museum in the world dedicated to a single artist.

→Edvard Munchs Plass 1, 0194
→23 49 35 00

<u>Sørenga Sjøbad</u>

This expansive seawater pool complex offers year-round aquatic enjoyment, catering even to those intrepid enough to brave the chilly waters of the Oslofjord in the heart of winter. But for those who prefer to eschew polar bear swims, it provides a sauna, promising to envelop visitors in warmth and steam.

→Sørengkaia 69, 0194

Holmenkollen Ski Tower

First opened in 1892, the tower has been frequently renovated to accommodate events like the Winter Olympics. There's the chance to see various events throughout the year and a museum there if you're interested in sports history. If you're feeling very adventurous, take the 361-metre-long zip line that takes you from the top of the jumping tower all the way down!

→Kongeveien 5, 0787
→91 67 19 47

KOK Oslo

Going to the sauna is a part of everyday life in Norway. In the Oslo Fjord, there are floating boat saunas with large windows offering views of the sea and the city. A skipper accompanies the guests and operates the boat.

→Langkaia 1, 1050
→93 40 05 22

T A S T E

Rest

Chef Jimmy Øien creates small masterpieces on the plates in the elegant restaurant dominated by wooden tables and dark walls. The key to his concept: all dishes are based on ingredients that are discarded in other fine-dining establishments, such as overly ripe bananas or crab shells

→Kirkegata 1-3, 0153
→92 25 00 16

Katla

Atli Mar Yngvasson takes an eclectic approach in his creations, combining flavours from Latin America and Asia with Nordic ingredients – Halibut Tostadas being one example. In a relaxed atmosphere, you can enjoy white wines, such as those from Germany, or one of the house's own Margarita creations alongside the meal.

→Universitetsgata 12, 0164
→22 69 50 00

Hot Shop

Contemporary 1 Michelin-star cuisine in a very laid-back setting. Jo Klakegg honed his craft at the legendary Noma and expands on it in the corner restaurant that used to be a sex toy shop. Set menu only.

→Københavngata 18, 0566
→46 67 37 18

Fuglen Coffee

A local coffee roaster with multiple locations in the city. Here in Northern Europe, coffee is comparatively lightly roasted, resulting in a less bitter taste and a somewhat more acidic flavour compared to Southern European preferences. In the main location, you can also find baked goods, and on Thursday evenings, they host live gigs

→St. Halvards gate 33, 0192
→92 16 56 12

The Little Pickle

English-inspired bistro cuisine with some pickled dishes, but certainly not limited to them. The atmosphere with its unfinished walls and understated wooden furniture is casual and uncomplicated, just like the cuisine. Don't forget to try the Picklebacks as well.

→Jens Bjelkes gate 9a, 0562
→41 22 28 39

Kuro Oslo

A charming little cafe - perfect for a relaxed start to the day. In addition to pastries from Tasty Munks and Ille Brød, there are also many gluten-free alternatives like Miso cookies. The young crew also knows what's happening around the city otherwise.

→Rathkes gate 9C, 0558
→45 32 32 51

Restaurant Hedone

Thai, but primarily Japanese cuisine, serves as the inspiration for this concept. To truly discover the diversity, it's best to indulge in the 9-course Omakase menu, where the high quality of Norway's fish and seafood products shines through.

→Skovveien 15, 0257
→22 12 05 02

A L'aise

A classic fine-dining establishment with French-inspired cuisine. Nothing here is funky or trendy, but everything is exceptionally well-prepared and refined. Their cheese cart is among the best in the city.

→Essendrops gate 6, 0368
→21 05 57 00

Holzweiler Platz Restaurant

The architecturally appealing environment continues inside the restaurant. The menu offers something for every taste. Guests are also welcome to stop by for a beer or coffee. Perfect for a pit stop during an architecture-inspired tour of the new neighbourhoods.

→Operagata 61D, 0194
→92 26 66 20

Le Benjamin bar & bistro

For those craving traditional bistro cuisine amidst all the Nordic cuisine, this is the right place. Oysters, tartare, along with a solid selection of wines from Burgundy and Bordeaux - here, they celebrate "la vie en rose" even during a long Norwegian winter.

→Søndre gate 6, 0550
→22 35 79 44

T O U C H

Moniker Oslo

The multi-brand store for modern luxury women's fashion. They offer the usual suspects for fashionistas, from Acne Studios to Yosuzi. Sometimes, the stylish staff takes themselves a bit too seriously

→Valkyriegata 3, 0366
→95 04 35 55

Kollekted By AS

A new curated store by the stylists Kråkvik&D´Orazio of FRAMA, this store is ground zero for the kind of minimalist, artistic pieces for which the brand is known. From textiles to perfume to furniture, you'll get the full experience at Kollekted By.

→Schous Plass 7 A, 0552
→40 04 27 43

f5 Concept Store

F5 Concept Store focuses on Norwegian designers, stocking everything from fashion to accessories to skincare. Brands like FWSS, Holzweiler and Sprekenhus line the shelves and the interior itself is a minimalist heaven.

→Rathkes gate 9, 0558
→94 11 93 17

Sorgenfri

A multi-level shop-space and concept gallery, this is also a place for unique art books. They stock exhibition catalogues, limited and rare editions, records, plus art objects, vintage furniture and sometimes even clothing. The attached cafe bar is also fun.

→Sorgenfrigata 16, 0365
→40 07 76 66

Norway Designs

With a huge collection of Norwegian, Scandinavian, and European everyday design items, this store is a no-frills place to start if you're looking to take home a piece of the city (or just love interior design). They often hold special exhibitions throughout the year.

→Lille Grensen 7, 0159
→23 11 45 10

S M E L L

Neseblod Records

Do you know about the "Turbojugend"? Norway has a huge rock and metal tradition, and this record store is among the best in the genre worldwide. It's also the right place to check out what the local music scene has to offer in this area.

→Schweigaards gate 56, 0656
→41 18 11 22

Merkur Bar

A cozy neighbourhood bar with a stylish retro wooden interior. In addition to classic cocktails and good wines, they also offer a selection of sake. Moreover, they serve small bites for those moments of hunger in between.

→Bjerregaards gate 5A, 0172
→91 24 93 17

Himkok Storgata Destilleri

With no sign outside and personnel behind the bar wearing labcoats, this is a spot for the cool kids. But their cocktails are no gimmick. The focus is on gin, vodka and aquavit, and the blends can be quite offbeat. We recommend the Caramelised Milk Cheese Brunets - yes, that's cheese in a cocktail and it's excellent.

→Storgata 27, 0184
→22 42 22 02

JÆGER

An open-air space, a pub, a dive bar, and a techno club - this place has many facets. So, it's worth checking out the program. The staff tends to be on the rougher side.

→Grensen 9, 0159

The Villa Oslo Dancing

A hedonistic dance temple with a long tradition in Oslo's nightlife: The venue is designed like a classic cellar club from the 1990s with a formidable sound system. On the second floor, you can sometimes discover interesting and offbeat sounds.

→Møllergata 23-25, 0179
→93 25 57 45

H E A R

F I L M

The Worst Person in the World, Joachim Trier, 2021

The third film in the director's Oslo trilogy, following Reprise (2006) and Oslo, August 31st (2011) it chronicles the life of Julie, on the verge of turning thirty, faced with a series of choices that force her to pursue new perspectives on her life in contemporary Oslo. Over the course of four years, she navigates love affairs and existential uncertainty as she starts deciding who she wants to become.

BORDEAUX

PARIS

“Paris is a collective masterpiece, perhaps the greatest in the world. Yet it is not a place for individual wonders, and many visitors may feel the kind of disappointment that I did on my first visit: of the world-famous attractions only the Eiffel Tower, the Opéra and the Louvre colonnade really live up to their reputation. But sooner or later, travelling from one piece of architecture to another, something quite different may catch your eye: a café, a public park, maybe nothing more than the gestures of a gendarme directing traffic. Then the magic will begin to work and may not stop until you are drunk with a hundred patches of gravel and a thousand expressive shrugs.”

Ian Nairn

S E E

Colonnes De Buren

A stroll under the arches of Le Jardin du Palais Royal is kind of a must if you're in town on a sunny day. It may be prime tourist territory, but there are still a few secret pockets of peace to be found.

→Galerie de la Cour d'Honneur, 2 Rue de Montpensier, 75001

Saint Sulpice

Saint Sulpice, one of Paris' grand churches, combines architectural beauty with a rich historical legacy. Its notable organ and Delacroix murals add layers of cultural significance.

→2 Rue Palatine, 75006
→01 46 33 21 78

Bourse du Commerce

Housed in Paris's distinguished Bourse de Commerce, renovated by architect Tadao Ando, the collection offers a unique intersection of contemporary art and historic architecture. Once a bustling grain exchange, this circular landmark, with its iconic dome, intertwines its mercantile past with a vibrant display of modern and contemporary artworks.

→2 Rue de Viarmes, 75001
→01 55 04 60 60

Musee des Arts Decoratifs

The Musee des Arts Decoratifs houses a comprehensive collection of decorative arts in Paris. It beautifully illustrates the influence and evolution of design and craft throughout history.

→107 Rue de Rivoli, 75001
→01 44 55 57 50

Palais de Tokyo

The “Disneyworld” of Paris’ art world offers just as much fun but on a slightly more intellectual level. A massive building invites guests to explore the thought-provoking—sometimes interactive—shows at their leisure. Definitely worth an afternoon.

→13 Av. du Président Wilson, 75116
→01 81 69 77 51

T A S T E

Vivant 2

Vivant 2 welcomes guests with an energetic soundtrack and friendly service, making its open kitchen bar a warm space rather than intimidating. Chef Rob Mendoza specializes in delicate, plant-centric dishes, with his innovative moles enhancing everything from broccoli to Bresse hen.

→43 R. des Petites Écuries, 75010
→09 67 49 96 26

Le Bougainville

A classic Bistro, in its timeless incarnation with neon lights and formica tables. It boasts the herring and potato salad and celery remoulade and the wines expected for a perfect pairing.

→5 Rue de la Banque, 75002
→01 42 60 05 19

Au Pied de Cochon

Au Pied de Cochon could not be more Parisian if it tried. From checkered tablecloths to the endless parade of pig prepared every which way, this is not so much a tourist trap as it is a glorious, still-relevant ode to the undying spirit of the French capital. Open 24 hours, seven days a week since its inauguration in 1946, the brasserie and its entire menu are a more than safe bet for those yearning for dinner at four in the morning.

→6 Rue Coquillière, 75001
→01 40 13 77 00

La Verre Vollé

La Verre Vollé, a wine bar in Paris, pairs carefully selected natural wines with simple, quality food. It's a reflection of the city's thriving natural wine movement.

→67 Rue de Lancry, 75010
→01 48 03 17 34

Le Servan

Run by a French cook, who works exclusively with fresh seasonal ingredients, the menu at Servan is small and to the point. Think Iberian black pork and razor clams with watercress, chickpea and hazelnuts or strawberries with almond and fennel. Make sure to browse the wine list and take on the lunch menu during the day as well.

→32 Rue Saint-Maur, 75011
→01 55 28 51 82

Bulot Bulot

Bulot Bulot is a seafood-centric restaurant, known for its fresh ingredients and inventive recipes.

→83 R. des Martyrs, 75018
→01 42 64 19 09

Le Baratin

Raquel Carena, an Argentine chef, is credited with pioneering bistronomy. Her retro bistro offers a personalized dining experience with a menu ranging from delicate to hearty dishes. The blackboard menu is enticing, prices are reasonable, and the wine selection is attractive. Reservations are highly recommended for this popular establishment.

→3 Rue Jouye-Rouve, 75020
→01 43 49 39 70

Café de Flore

One of the oldest and most prestigious cafés in the city, in the heart of Saint-Germain-des-Prés. Café de Flore attracts a colourful bunch of characters—old men enjoy their café with the newspaper while stylish shoppers take a break from perusing the fancy stores on Boulevard Saint-Germain. All while tourists pose for pictures in front of the iconic entrance.

→172 Bd Saint-Germain, 75006
→01 45 48 55 26

Freddys

Freddys, a wine bar and small plates spot. The menu includes grilled eggplant with hazelnuts, pomegranate, and cilantro, miso-glazed salmon mi-cuit, and mouthwatering duck heart skewers. They also offer a variety of cheeses and charcuterie. A bar-only restaurant, it doesn't take reservations so show up there leave your name and have a drink at the surrounding bars in St Germain.

→54 Rue de Seine, 75006

La Cave a Michel

Questioned about the concept behind his beloved neighbourhood wine bar and eatery, Chef Romain Tischenko said it was “just a place to grab a drink and some food.” But don’t be fooled—the three square-metre kitchen sees things like black angus marrying anchovies, or chocolate ganache linking up with olive oil. All the matches are made in heaven, as are the natural wines meant to go along with them.

→36 Rue Sainte-Marthe, 75010
→01 42 45 94 47

T O U C H

Maison Courtot

Maison Courtot epitomizes the craftsmanship of Parisian haberdashery. This bespoke shirtmaker continues a time-honored tradition.

→113 Rue de Rennes, 75006
→01 45 48 54 86

Puces de Saint Ouen

The Puces de Saint Ouen, one of the largest antique markets in the world.

→110 Rue des Rosiers, 93400

Isaac Reina

Isaac Reina, a Parisian leather goods store. Trained at Hermes. Reina produces his small leather goods from Italian tanneries from small artisans in the outskirts of Paris.

→12 Rue de Thorigny, 75003
→01 42 78 81 95

Librairie Yvon Lambert

This is the place for unique art books. The space also stocks exhibition catalogues, limited and rare editions, DVDs, records, art objects, and prints.

→14 Rue des Filles du Calvaire, 75003
→01 45 66 55 84

Ofr

Ofr. functions as both a gallery and bookstore or library of intriguing magazines. They have frequent events and exhibitions—so pop in and ask, or check it out online. Their expansive mode of being has led to various locations around the world, including Tokyo, but this is where it all started.

→20 Rue Dupetit-Thouars, 75003

S M E L L

Le Bar Rue du Dragon

A bar needs a nice atmosphere. Here you can expect red velvet carpeting, leopard print bar stools, a great aquarium, an able bartender who will gladly debate with you the latest Besson film and a good atmosphere which can make you believe you want to spend the rest of your days at this place.

→34 Rue du Dragon, 75006
→01 43 25 87 67

Cercle Suedois

Cercle Suedois, a private Swedish club in Paris, offers a taste of Scandinavian culture in the heart of the city. It hosts a Jazz night on Wednesdays and is both connected to the dynamite through Nobel and the aborted plan to blow up the city during the Second World War.

→242 Rue de Rivoli Esc.A 2ème étage, 75001
→01 42 60 76 67

Chez Georges

Chez Georges, a beloved wine bar in Paris, reflects the city's vibrant social scene where the spirit of Django Reinhardt remains. It hosts a Manouche Jazz night on Tuesdays.

→1 Rue du Mail, 75002
→01 42 60 07 11

Silencio

David Lynch's club is one of the city's most exclusive places to party, evidenced by a glut of artists and stars enjoying a late-night affair. It strikes a fine balance between nightclub and bar, and the atmosphere is just as mesmerising as its aesthetics.

→142 Rue Montmartre, 75002

Rex Club

Inaugurated by Laurent Garnier in 1992, the Rex Club stands as one of Paris's most venerable venues, perpetuating the pulsating beats of techno and house for over three decades. Balancing a luminous stage, wall-lined booths and seating, and a sprawling dance floor that reaches the bar, it curates a versatile nightlife experience for avid clubbers across the city.

→5 Bd Poissonnière, 75002
→01 42 36 10 96

H E A R

F I L M

Diva, Jean-Jacques Beineix, 1981

A young opera lover becomes embroiled in a twisted web of crime and passion in Paris, after inadvertently recording a performance by his favorite diva. This stylish thriller helped establish the Cinéma du look movement in France.

PORTO

“Porto-Cidade, beautiful woman. She only loves who she wants! Distant blonde, frigid lover, who screams with passion: It’s São João!”

Arnaldo Trindade

S E E

Serralves Museum

The Serralves Museum, designed by architect Álvaro Siza Vieira, serves as a notable platform for contemporary art. Visitors encounter a thoughtful array of artworks, such as those by Olafur Eliasson and Helena Almeida, within a building celebrated for its minimalist architectural eloquence.

→R. Dom João de Castro 210, 4150-417
→22 615 6500

Galeria Oitavo

This art gallery is literally inside its co-founders' apartment, which in itself defies the perceived boundaries between personal space and what an exhibition space should be. For the shows, they invite a group of artists to work

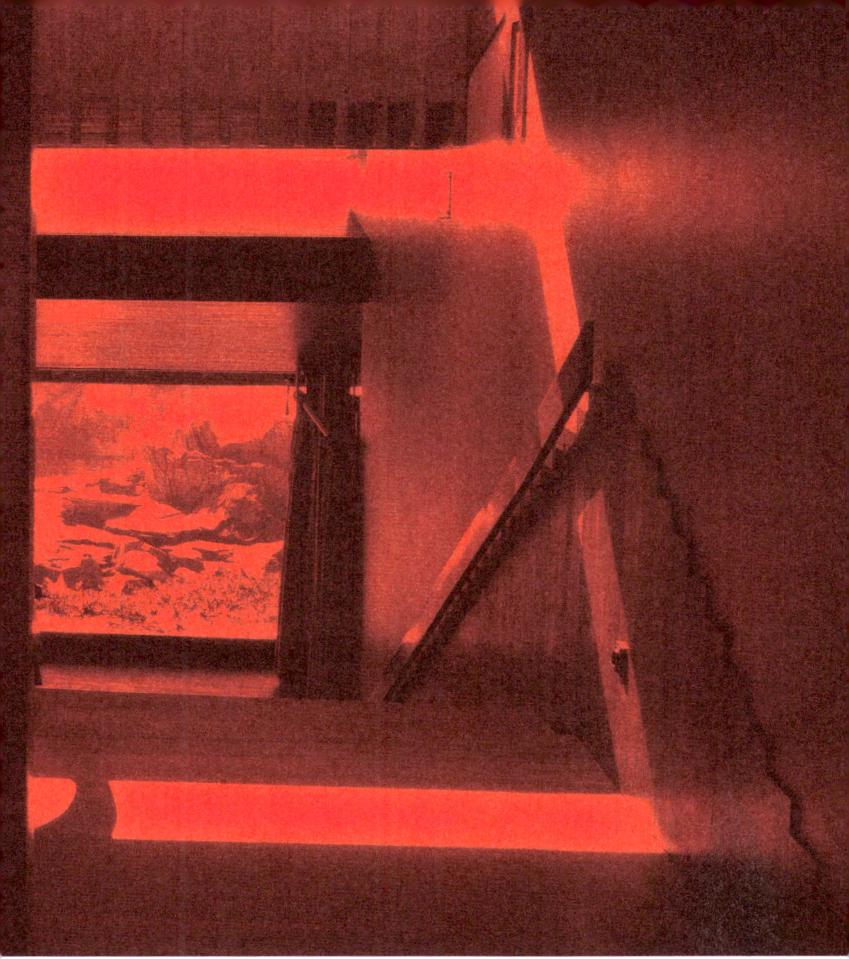

on the same theme, as a medium to self and outer discovery. Reach them through email to book a visit.

→Rua da Alegria 582, 8°, Dto. F, 4000-037
→914 086 346

Piscina das Mares

Piscina das Marés, a remarkable seaside pool complex in Leça da Palmeira, Portugal, is a masterful design by the acclaimed architect Álvaro Siza Vieira. With its organic forms seamlessly interweaving with the rocky coastline, the pools provide a unique intersection of natural and man-made environments.

→Av. Liberdade, 4450-716
→22 995 2610

Casa da Musica

Casa da Música, a distinctive concert hall situated in, emanates the inventive design prowess of Dutch architect Rem Koolhaas. Acting as a cultural epicentre, the venue resonates with diverse musical notes, from classical to contemporary genres, within its innovative and multifaceted spaces.

→Av. da Boavista 604-610, 4149-071
→22 012 0220

Rivoli Teatro Municipal

Rivoli Theatre in Porto, a beacon of cultural expression and performing arts, stands with a rich history dating back to its opening in 1913. Throughout the decades, this beloved venue has hosted a myriad of performances, from cinema to live theatre, becoming an integral part of the city's cultural tapestry. Today, the Rivoli continues to embrace diverse artistic presentations, fostering a space where traditional and contemporary arts coalesce.

→R. do Bonjardim 143, 4000-440
→22 339 2200

T A S T E

Salta o Muro

Close to Matosinhos' fish auction, this rustic restaurant serves fresh grilled fish with daily changing house specials that always attract plenty of locals. The space fills up quickly and the restaurant doesn't take reservations, so get there early for lunch or dinner if you don't like waiting around while the scents of grilled fish drive you mad.

→R. Heróis de França 386, 4450-155
→22 938 0870

Gazela

Famous old spot serving cachorrinhos (little hot dogs with two different sausages bought at the local Bolhão Market) with melted cheese. They come sliced in tiny bits, so you can eat them with a toothpick while slurping on a beer. After Anthony Bourdain visited this spot and made it even more famous, they opened a second venue right across the street.

→Tv. do Cimo de Vila 4, 4000-434
→22 112 4981

Casa Guedes

An oldie run by a family who stayed true to their simple classics with a menu based on Portuguese staple ingredients—cheeses, cured meats, bread and white wines. But what really makes locals stand in a queue is their pork sandwiches filled with molten Portuguese cheese from Serra da Estrela.

→Praça dos Poveiros 130, 4000-393
→22 200 2874

Elemento

The chef boldly embraces fundamental culinary techniques here, utilizing wood as the exclusive cooking medium on the grill and in the oven. The offerings delve into traditional Portuguese cuisine, all while infusing a contemporary twist.

→Rua do Almada 51, 4050-036
→22 492 8193

Apego

Run by a French cook, who works exclusively with fresh seasonal ingredients, the menu at Apege is small and to the point. Think Iberian black pork and razor clams with watercress, chickpea and hazelnuts or strawberries with almond and fennel. Make sure to browse the wine list and take on the lunch menu during the day as well.

→R. de Santa Catarina 1198, 4000-457
→22 550 0457

Majestic Café

Majestic Café, a historic café in Porto, offers a journey back in time with its belle époque decor. It's a symbol of the city's longstanding café culture.

→R. de Santa Catarina 112, 4000-442
→22 200 3887

Cafe Vitoria

Café Vitória, nestled in one of the well-known streets of the heartwarming city, stands as a little treasure amidst the urban setting. Though renowned as a café, it hides a delightful secret on its upper floor: a restaurant that emanates a genuinely comfortable and relaxed ambiance, contrasting the bustling café/bar below.

→R. de Cedofeita 622, 4050-176
→22 200 9698

Casa de Cha da Boa Nova

At this Siza-designed restaurant, perched above Praia da Boa Nova, the idea of “bringing the sea to your table” takes on an authentic flair as waves nearly caress the dining space, situating diners just a breath away from the ocean’s majesty. Nested within a nationally recognized monument, Chef Rui Paula crafts cuisine that draws inspiration from a verse (“hitherto unchartered waters”) penned by esteemed Portuguese poet Luís Vaz de Camões in his magnum opus, The Lusiads.

→Av. Liberdade 1681, 4450-718
→22 994 0066

Esquina do Avesso

Nestled in the picturesque Leça da Palmeira, Esquina do Avesso provides an enchanting culinary journey, effortlessly blending traditional flavours with modern, inventive techniques. Guests can expect a tapestry of vibrant dishes, such as the delicately constructed lasagna of duck and aesthetically delightful desserts, all curated under the skilled hands of Chef Nuno Castro.

→R. Santa Catarina 102, 4450-631
→912 286 521

T O U C H

Louie Louie

One of the most iconic vinyl stores in town with that classic retro feel. Perfect if you’re looking to hear something made in Porto, the independent music shop provides a great selection that ranges from disco to jazz, punk to Portuguese fado.

→Rua do Almada 536, 4050-034
→22 201 0384

Casa Almada

A reference for anyone who enjoys vintage or straight-to-the-point furniture design. The shop spans two floors of designer pieces and old findings. Susana, the owner, has designed some of the pieces herself and she can guide you through everything in the store. And yes, they do ship overseas.

→Rua do Almada 544, 4050-034
→918 226 205

Coracao Alecrim

Coracao Alecrim is a concept store in Porto offering a range of clothing, accessories and home goods all with a focus on sustainable and ethically made products.

→Tv. de Cedofeita 28, 4050-183
→912 958 073

Mercado do Bolhao

Established on a site purchased by the town hall in 1839 and named after an air bubble ("bolha") formed by a creek running through its square, the market's current neoclassical structure dates back to 1914, with distinct areas for fishmongers, butchers, greengrocers, and florists spread across two floors. The lively environment is animated by vendors' distinct "pregão" (outcry), a compelling trade call, and an uncommon sight of a mobile knife sharpener at its northern entrance. Bolhão captivates visitors with an authentic Portuguese experience, offering a peek into everyday life, and culinary traditions like the exclusive "floury tripes".

→R. Formosa 322, 4000-248
→22 332 6024

S M E L L

Passos Manuel

Once a renowned cabaret and exotic parlour, the club has undergone a transformation into a prominent and all-embracing establishment within the underground scene. With high-quality bookings that include international names like James Talbot and Daniel Haksman, as well as national legends like Yen Sung, it has solidified its reputation.

→Rua de Passos Manuel nº 137

Perola Negra Club

The Perola Negra Club in Porto conjures a vibrant and eclectic nightlife experience for its attendees. With a storied past that pulses through its walls, the venue has metamorphosed from a notorious strip club in the 70s to a contemporary nightclub, maintaining its retro charm and sassy spirit.

→Rua de Gonçalo Cristóvão 284, 4000-145

Maus Habitos

Maus Hábitos, translating to "Bad Habits" in English, is a dynamic space in Porto that seamlessly blends art, culture, and culinary experiences. Situated in a building with a retro charm, it provides a vibrant backdrop to a myriad of activities and events, from alternative music gigs and DJ nights to art exhibitions and film screenings.

→R. de Passos Manuel 178 4º Piso, 4000-382
→937 202 918

Candelabro

Part secondhand bookstore, part lively bar, grab a book (mostly about cinema and photography) from the shelves and hang out at one of the tables reading and sipping wine. In the evenings things get a bit more lively, as the city's artsy crowd arrives to take their pick from the cocktail menu and converse about rather pressing intellectual matters.

→Rua da Conceição 3, 4050-215

H E A R

FILM

Porto of My Childhood, Manoel de Oliveira, 2001

Portuguese filmmaking legend Manoel de Oliveira, renowned for his distinctive blend of freedom and precision, revisited Porto, his birthplace, at the age of ninety-three to create this deeply moving documentary collage. This film captures the essence of Porto as he remembered it from his childhood—a city steeped in history and bustling with artists and intellectuals.

ROMA M2
9843

ROME

“Rome reminds me of a man who lives by exhibiting to travellers his grandmother’s corpse.”

James Joyce

S E E

The Baths of Caracalla

The Baths of Caracalla, remnants of Rome's ancient splendour, offer a peek into a bygone era of opulence and communal social life. Visitors wander amidst the towering columns and intricate mosaics of this extensive bath complex, immersing themselves in the architectural grandeur and social culture of 3rd-century Rome.

→Viale delle Terme di Caracalla, 00153
→06 3996 7702

Villa Medici

The Villa Medici, gracefully perched upon the Pincian Hill in Rome, elegantly unites art, history, and exquisite gardens. With its rich tapestry of Renaissance architecture and lush landscapes, this villa, now the French Academy in Rome, provides a serene yet culturally rich retreat, intertwining the creative energies of resident artists and

scholars with the indelible historical echoes of its walls and walkways. Accommodation offering rooms with views over the garden are available booked via email 2 months in advance.

→Viale della Trinità dei Monti, 1, 00187
→06 67611

Nuovo Sacher

Cinephiles flock to this old-school movie theatre, originally built in the 1930s to provide affordable entertainment to the working class of Trastevere and Testaccio. Now owned by award-winning filmmaker Nanni Moretti, the single-screen cinema shows indie films and offbeat classics throughout the day. Quirky to the core, the retro concessions stand even stocks a rich chocolate sacher cake as a reference to the cinema's name.

→Largo Ascianghi, 1, 00153
→06 581 8116

Hendrik Christian Anderson Museum

Housing the Norwegian-American sculptor's enthralling creations, from evocative sculptures to intriguing architectural models and drawings. Nestled within a charming villa, the museum immerses visitors in Andersen's imaginative world, revealing his aspirations of building an ideal city filled with monumental architecture and evocative artistic expressions.

→Via Pasquale Stanislao Mancini, 20, 00196
→06 321 9089

Parco degli Acquedotti

One of Rome's most underexplored outdoor spaces, the ruins running through this public park in suburban Rome offer a taste of its ancient grandeur. Virtually tourist-free, locals know that this section of Parco dell'Appia Antica is an ideal spot for enjoying the mild local weather or renting a bike to cycle past the massive and well-preserved aqueducts that cut across green hills.

→Via Lemonia, 00174
→06 513 5316

Palazzo della Civiltà Italiana

In Turin's porticos, Nietzsche perceived a spiritual power, while De Chirico recognized a profound, poetic essence. Unlike Germany or Russia, where architectural styles disappeared with the fall of political movements, Italy experienced a continuum that allowed architects like Aldo Rossi to flourish and perpetuate the beloved arches. It is in EUR, the location of the 1942 World Fair which was never held (as certain other events intervened), that the neoclassical building laid unfinished and abandoned. Now revitalized as a modern business district, the Palazzo has been repurposed to accommodate the Fendi headquarters.

→Quadrato della Concordia, 00144

T A S T E

Checchino 1887

This family-operated venue, which was initiated as a wine bar, welcomes guests in its warm, wood-panelled space. While its origins are in its well-curated, sensibly priced wine offerings, the culinary experience boldly champions offal, presenting dishes like veal head with citrus and beef tripe cooked in pecorino.

→Via di Monte Testaccio, 30, 00153
→333 585 5055

Salumeria Roscioli Restaurant

Brothers Alessandro and Pierluigi Roscioli transformed the family grocery store into a refined bottega with a kitchen and wine cellar. Here patrons can sample what is probably the finest classic Roman dishes made with fierce attention to the product sourced. Part of a mini-empire in Rome, make sure to check out the Antico Forno (bakery) and Caffe next door.

→Via dei Giubbonari, 21, 00186
→06 687 5287

Armando Al Pantheon

Opening for business in 1961 as a wine shop with a small kitchen, family-run Armando al Pantheon has slowly evolved into a white tablecloth affair. The small dining room around the corner from the Pantheon is packed with a mix of local businessmen and well-heeled visitors. The menu is traditionally Roman, with refined takes on classics like spaghetti all'amatriciana, artichokes alla romana, and an excellent oxtail.

→Salita de' Crescenzi, 31, 00186

Ai Marmi

The line out the door of this traditional pizzeria sometimes gives the old-fashioned eatery the same lively feel as Rome's hottest nightclub. But the crowd is well-managed and satiated by the hundreds of crispy thin-crust pizzas that emerge from the wood-fired oven every night. While the

Margherita is hard to beat, one of the pizzeria's specialties comes topped with fresh zucchini blossoms and savoury sausage.

→Viale di Trastevere, 53-59, 00153
→06 580 0919

Rimessa Roscioli

Part of the Roscioli family, Rimessa provides with some of the best past in Rome but focuses on the wine pairings. Over 2,500 bottles, let the very knowledgeable staff, (ciao Gae) guide you on this journey through local, international, classic and natural wines.

→Via del Conservatorio, 58, 00186
→06 6880 3914

Roma Sparita

On one of his many trips to Rome, Anthony Bourdain visited this place for lunch without sharing the address... As we are not on primetime CNN we decided to do so, as this is one of the finest Caccio e Peppe one can have, served in a (cheesy, but delicious) cheese bowl, it is best enjoyed paired with a cold white Grillo seated outside overlooking the piazza.

→Piazza di Santa Cecilia, 24, 00153
→06 580 0757

Rocco Ristorante

Rocco, a classic Roman trattoria, offers a laid-back ambiance amidst a polished decor and a menu of exquisite pasta and fresh seafood, displayed on an elementary school-style blackboard. It maintains a cozy balance between a grand and a casual dining experience, accommodating patrons in a single dinner seating.

→Via Giovanni Lanza, 93, 00184
→06 487 0942

Forno Campo de' Fiori

Forno Campo de' Fiori, a vibrant bakery in a lively market square, is renowned for its simple pizza slices, sold by weight amidst a bustling, no-frills atmosphere. Despite its lack of seating, locals and tourists alike flock for the convenience and delectable offerings like pizza rossa and pizza bianca. Situated near Piazza Navona, it's a must-visit for a quick, authentic Roman slice during your city center explorations, whether for breakfast, lunch, or a late afternoon snack.

→Campo de' Fiori, 22, 00186
→06 6880 6662

Checco Er Carettiere

Checco er Carettiere in Trastevere offers a simple yet authentic Roman culinary experience with its menu, emphasizing fresh, locally sourced ingredients and staple Roman dishes, such as carbonara or Carciofi alla giudia. Come for the tavern-style ambience where the long tables and wood-panelling and you'll understand why it's been frequented by trasteverini, poets and fashion designers.

→Via Benedetta, 10, 00153
→06 581 7018

T O U C H

Gammarelli

The official tailor of the Pope. Opened in 1798, it has been held by the same family for 6 generations. Entering the shop you may be perusing the fine garments alongside a Roman cardinal or two up-and-coming bishops from Idaho. For those of us who hold a not-so-holy position in the catholic world, they make great socks.

→Via di S. Chiara, 34, 00186
→06 6880 1314

Trionfale Market

The light airy decor of this shop will make you forget you're in a vintage store at all. The racks are colour-coded and neatly arranged, perfect for finding your next special item.

→Via Andrea Doria, 00192

Antica Libreria Cascianelli

All'Antica Libreria Cascianelli, one of Rome's historic bookshops, is a haven for collectors, offering prints, artworks, antiques, and rare books. Maintaining its décor virtually unchanged since the early 19th century, it features a door leading to secret rooms, imbuing the space with an air of mystery and historical charm.

→Largo Febo, 15, 00186
→348 863 0220

Eataly

The department store is a mecca for Italian cuisine enthusiasts. This large food hall and market offers a diverse selection of Italy's best foods and culinary products from all regions, reflecting the country's gastronomic richness and diversity.

→Piazzale 12 Ottobre 1492, 00154
→02 0999 7900

S M E L L

Club Derriere

Club Derrière, a bohemian speakeasy, immerses visitors in a dark, moody atmosphere with its unfinished walls, exposed pipes, and jazz ambiance. The clientele, drawn by the secretive vibe and expertly crafted cocktails, embraces the drama of the low lighting and meticulous drink presentations. While the emphasis is on innovative cocktail creations, like the Floral and Vanity or English Pie, dining is not the focus—though adjacent Osteria Delle Copelle offers food if needed.

→Vicolo delle Coppelle, 59, 00186
→329 045 2505

Litro

This wine bar distinguishes itself with an array of natural and biodynamic wines, alongside classic Italian and inventive mezcal or rum-based cocktails. While the focus is on the meticulously selected drinks, the food—ranging from cured meats and cheeses to smoked-chicken-and-guacamole panini—complements the beverage offerings

→Via Fratelli Bonnet, 5, 00152
→06 4544 7639

Goa Club

From its days as a motorcycle repair shop to the current techno club iteration, this Ostiense venue has managed to keep it dirty and urban. The name is a nod to moonlight parties on Indian beaches, which is echoed by the eclectic and vaguely colonial décor. Well-known DJs regularly stop by and orchestrate massive dance parties over the high-tech Audio Factory sound system.

→Via Giuseppe Libetta, 13, 00154
→06 574 8277

Drink Kong

Mixologist Patrick Pistolesi's first solo venture was bound to become a success. The neon-light-decorated imbibing den is just a cool place to drink some very good cocktails, and because of that, you'll sometimes have a hard time getting through the door. But it's worth it to mingle with Rome's cool kids and, depending on the day, listen to some live music.

→Piazza di S. Martino Ai Monti, 8, 00154
→06 2348 8666

H E A R

F I L M

Caro Diario, Nanni Moretti, 1993

This introspective Italian comedy-drama, divided into three chapters, is a semi-autobiographical reflection on life, love, and art. Its director and lead actor, Nanni Moretti, uses the film as a diary to explore aspects of his life and thoughts on contemporary society.

STOCKHOLM

“Stockholm is surely an urban planner’s dream. Everything works. Everything looks good.”

Janine di Giovanni

S E E

Artipelag

Shrouded by pine trees on the island of Värmdö, Artipelag is just 20 minutes from Stockholm centre. Eschew the roads in favour of a boat: sailing into the heart of the archipelago is an experience, chiming with the gallery's credo of combining art and nature. Johan Nyrén's magnificent building covers over 10,000 square metres, and hosts a broad range of exhibitions, showcasing artists from Tracey Emin to Candida Höfer. But the oeuvre isn't limited to the walls—rising through the floor of the café is a two billion-year-old metamorphic gneiss rock, and the surrounding views and boardwalks speak for themselves.

→Artipelagstigen 1, 134 40
→08-570 130 00

Skinnarviksparken

Skinnarviksparken, located by Skinnarviksberget, boasts Stockholm's highest natural point at 53 meters above sea level, offering breathtaking views over Riddarfjärden and the city. The park features a blend of untouched nature and manicured spaces, with historical wooden houses from the 1700s. Historically, tanners lived here due to the unpleasant olfactory emanations from their work.

→Skinnarbacken, 117 27
→08-508 120 00

Fotografiska

On top of a stellar cafe that overlooks the entire city, Fotografiska is one of the best museums in Stockholm. They host 4 major and dozens of minor photography exhibitions per year, plus workshops, talks, and other events. It is a dazzling place.

→Stadsgårdshamnen 22, 116 45
→08-509 005 00

Skogskyrkogården

An early-20th-century cemetery celebrated for its thoughtful landscape and architectural design. The UNESCO heritage site blends the natural backdrop of pine trees, gravel, and gentle hills with purposefully designed chapels, a crematorium, and a notable granite cross. All while preserving the Nordic tradition of simplicity.

→Sockenvägen
→08-508 317 30

Liljevalchs Konsthall

Sitting pretty on the island of Djurgården, this attractive gallery space was designed by the renowned Carl Bergsten and is a sure crowd-pleaser for art lovers. It was the first independent public museum for contemporary art in Sweden—and it has a great store, too.

→Djurgårdsvägen 60, 115 21
→08-508 313 30

T A S T E

Rolfs Kök

This institution of modern Stockholm gastronomy mixes up the European classic flavours in a bustling and casual dining room. The interior was designed by local artists, and the counter is the place to be if you'd like to see the dynamic owner-chef in action.

→Tegnérgatan 41, 111 61
→08-10 16 96

Black Milk Gastro Bar

In the evening, BMGB offers a fusion of traditional Japanese omakase with global flair, an intimate cocktail bar serving small dishes and for lunch, old school cooking with Southern European influences.

→Engelbrektsgatan 3, 114 32
→08-611 80 18

Bord

Central to the setting is a communal table, complemented by a few intimate tables and counter seating. The daily Mediterranean-inspired menu showcases straightforward dishes, with starters seamlessly transitioning into mains. Exceptional cooking highlights the premium ingredients; try the wood-fired oven turbot if available.

→Roslagsgatan 43, 113 54
→08-91 40 88

Sturehof

This place has been around for a long time: first as a German Beer Hall founded in 1897, and then in its current iteration as a seafood restaurant from 1905. The menu is a French-meets-Swedish extravaganza of fresh ingredients, indulgent dishes and an upscale-meets-casual atmosphere.

→Stureplan 2, 114 35
→08-440 57 30

Lillebrors Bageri

Around the world people are lining up for bread, but unlike war-torn countries or for reasons of societal collapse, the lineups here are a testament to the quality of the products.

→Rörstrandsgatan 10, 113 40

Brutalisten

Founded by German conceptual artist Carsten Höller, this captivating restaurant follows the principles of the 'Brutalist Kitchen Manifesto'. The menu categorizes dishes into 'Orthodox Brutalist', 'Brutalist', and 'Semi Brutalist', reflecting the extent to which one wants to experience the essence of pristine ingredients without any sauces or additions. To quote from their manifesto: Brutalist Cuisine is not about lack of sophistication, but lack of combination of different ingredients and a commitment to purity.

→Regeringsgatan 71, 111 56
→072-161 86 83

Frantzén

Of all the fine dining restaurants in the area this one could probably be identified as the big-name bully. Michelin-starred chef de cuisine Björn Frantzen's everyday effort is sure to keep it that way for the time being. If you want some spectacle with your food, choose to sit at the kitchen counter.

→Klara Norra kyrkogata 26, 111 22
→08-20 85 80

Restaurant Konstnärsbaren

Since its inception in 1931, Konstnärsbaren, translating to "the artist bar," has been a cherished gem in Stockholm's culinary landscape. Adorned with artworks from notable artists like Isaac Grünewald and Einar Forseth, this relaxed and artistic venue serves traditional Swedish husmanskost, focusing on meat and potatoes, but also offering vegetarian choices.

→Smålandsgatan 7, 111 46
→08-679 60 32

Tennstopet

This old-school eatery serves Swedish cuisine so traditional, it's exotic. Herring and salmon are a year-round staple, but pop in during spring for a taste of crow—or maybe some Christmas-time stockfish? The hunters' luck determines the menu, which is as real as it gets.

→Dalagatan 50, 113 24
→08-32 25 18

T O U C H

Svenskt Tenn

The store began with a meeting between two individuals with innovative ideas: the stylist and businesswoman Estrid Ericsson and the designer Josef Frank. Their distinctive patterned and brightly colored creations feature modern designs, a gift department with glass, pottery, and objects by upcoming established designers. Note the expensive concave window that Estrid Ericson, the founder of the company, had specially delivered from London against everyone's advice but succeeded in intriguing passersby to this day.

→Strandvägen 5, 114 51
→08-670 16 00

Nitty Gritty

Nitty Gritty is a multi-brand boutique that carries some of the best Swedish and international brands around. Everything is highly curated and beautifully styled. This store is womenswear and accessories; right next door is their men's store!

→Krukmakargatan 24-26, 118 51
→08-658 24 40

Centralbadet

This bathhouse is located in a beautiful art nouveau building with a courtyard from 1909, where architect Wilhelm Klemming materialized his dream of an "open window to nature."

→Drottninggatan 88, 111 36
→08-545 213 00

Public Service Gallery

Located in a former bank in Östermalmstorg, the gallery, after extensive renovations, spans 300 sqm over two floors, designed by Halleroeds. The trio, with diverse backgrounds from international art institutions to business, aims to introduce emerging global artists to a Scandinavian audience, fostering collaborative engagements with institutions and artists.

→Storgatan 1, 114 44

Östermalms Saluhall

Established in 1888, Östermalms Saluhall is an iconic food hall cherished by locals and tourists alike. Crafted by young architects, Isak Gustaf Clason and Kasper Salin, inspired by their travels to North Germany, Italy, and France. This influence can be seen in the hall's intricate brickwork and cast-iron structures, reminiscent of France's majestic Eiffel Tower. With 18 dedicated traders, many boasting generational ties to the hall, visitors can expect a blend of tradition, quality, and heartfelt service.

→Östermalmstorg 31, 114 39

S M E L L

Lucy's Flower Shop

To access this hidden gem in Stureplan, you'll require a door code (or a booking online), adding to the allure. Lucy's, a lavish speakeasy renowned for its exquisite cocktails, attracts the fashion crowd, making it a favoured destination for late-night relaxation.

→Birger Jarlsgatan 20, 114 34

Huset Under Bron

This club has expanded well beyond its eponymous "House Under A Bridge" to a fully-fledged nightclub, radio, gallery, festival, label and vegetarian restaurant displaying what (in their words) "creativity, love, alcohol (and a bit of robbery) can do.

→Hammarby Slussväg 2, 118 60
→08-644 20 23

Coquetel Social

Permissive and decadent are the two words that best describe this bar near the Stureplan public square. The interior loves the luxury of the 1960s and harks back to the glory days of Rio de Janeiro and Havana. Classic cocktails made with the best ingredients are the reason why people keep coming back for more, as well as the good-looking crowd.

→Birger Jarlsgatan 20, 114 34

Rumble/Sway

Blending the vibrancy of a bar with the allure of a nightclub, a space where cocktails shine, yet an expansive wine and beer selection beckons. Their unique bottle locker concept adds a personal touch, allowing patrons to enjoy their spirits at their leisure.

→Birger Jarlsgatan 33, 111 45
→08-611 22 22

Hosoi Listening Bar

A Swedish take on the Japanese listening bar, Hosoi boasts two distinct rooms. One to “Eat Drink” foods based on Japanese Otsumami and Swedish culinary traditions, the other to “Dance Listen” to a diverse lineup both local and international. Be on the lookout for their multi-genre music festival which takes place in the backyard of the area Slakthusområdet once a year.

→Förbindelsehallen, 121 62

H E A R

F I L M

Summer with Monika, Ingmar Bergman, 1953

Lesser known but hugely influential among the master's oeuvre, this is the story of two working-class teenagers who flee Stockholm on an amorous adventure. It influenced the cliché of Sweden as an erotic paradise

VIENNA

“Shattered into pieces
In the peace of the night.
While a bird above us
Laughs at us.
My last wish: Idyll
Falco said once.
Vienna is everything
And the emperor is nothing”

Thees Uhlmann

S E E

Belvedere 21

After the arrival of the new century, the former 20er Haus was carefully modernised and remodelled by Adolf Krischanitz—and renamed 21er Haus. It's now a branch of the nearby Belvedere Museums and houses the stunning 1950s-era Blickle Kino.

→Arsenalstraße 1, 1030
→01 795570

Wotrubakirche

Entering the Wotruba Church is rather like immersing yourself in a work of art. That's because it was designed by a sculptor. Inspired by the Chartres Cathedral, Viennese Fritz Wotruba used 152 blocks of concrete in its construction. The monument embodies the experimental side of Vienna—rough and asymmetrical, yet entrenched in tradition.

→Ottillingerpl. 1, 1230
→01 8886147

Burggarten

The grassy lawns of the Burggarten offer an ideal place to kick back and enjoy the simplest pleasures of life—sunshine, good company, birds chirping and the top-notch coffee served on premises.

→Josefsplatz 1, 1010

TBA21

TBA21, or Thyssen-Bornemisza Art Contemporary, situates itself prominently within the Vienna art scene, presenting contemporary art and thought in a nuanced dialogue with its visitors. The institution is housed within the beautiful Augarten and is known for fostering projects and exhibitions that traverse a broad spectrum of disciplines, from the visual arts to thought-provoking environmental dialogues around ecology, sustainability, and the role of art in society.

→Köstlergasse 1, 1060
→01 51398560

Strandbad Gänsehäufel

This lido on the banks of an old arm of the Danube blends a beautiful natural setting with the distant view of skyscrapers in the Viennese business district.

→Moissigasse 21, 1220
→01 2699016

T A S T E

Restaurant Steirereck

A true culinary institution in Vienna, it's rumoured Steirereck is receiving its third Michelin star sometime soon. Not a surprise, considering how innovative the cuisine at this avant-garde restaurant is. Modern, clear design meets the creative cuisine of Heinz Reitbauer, who prepares regional products with utmost precision and sophistication. The bread and cheese cart shouldn't be missed.

→Am Heumarkt 2A, 1030
→01 7133168

Gasthaus Wolf

Creative Austrian cuisine in an unpretentious atmosphere. The value for money here is outstanding, as well as the ingredients used in dishes on the weekly-changing menu. The chefs are famous for their "from-brain-to-bone" approach, so get ready to try delicacies like roasted veal liver or baked bull's testicles.

→Große Neugasse 20, 1040
→0664 1423452

Café Korb

Vienna sure knows how to preserve its historic coffeehouses—and Korb is no exception. Drop by for a coffee, some strudel and a game of Kegel, the Austrian version of bowling.

→Brandstätte 7/9, 1010

Café Central

Madrid's most respected jazz spot is set on a quiet central square in this attractive barrio. A classic jazz café, complete with high ceilings, antique pillars and small tables, it's open every night until 2:30 am. Check the roster of international jazz talents and book ahead.

→Herrengasse 14, 1010
→01 5333763

Zum schwarzen Kameel

Soaked in Austrian tradition, this restaurant dates back to

1618 when Johann Baptist Cameel opened a store for exotic spices. Rub shoulders with the spirits of former patrons like Ludwig van Beethoven and enjoy some typical Austrian cuisine, like the house specialty "Beinschinken" (ham on the bone).

→Bognergasse 5, 1010
→01 5338125

Café Ansari

Nestled on the quiet end of Praterstrasse, this couple-owned restaurant offers food that could best be described as Georgian-Oriental. Stylish yet laid-back, the emphasis here is on the details—everything from the tableware to the food and presentation is thoughtfully considered.

→Praterstraße 15, 1020
→01 2765102

Joseph Brot

This popular brunch and coffee spot offers a sit-down option or upscale takeaway experience. Owner Josef Weghaupt only uses ingredients from local producers he personally knows, so there's a definite freshness guarantee. If you're looking to pick up and go, the sandwiches are definitely recommended.

→Landstraßer Hauptstraße 4, 1030
→01 7102881

Kaiserzeit Würstelstand

The kiosk dates back to 1909 but has been operating as a Würstelstand since 1990. The "Kaiserzeit" sausage stand, now infused with historical and culinary nuances, serves classics like Viennese soup pot and kettle goulash, ensuring the legacy of traditional Austrian fast food continues with a dash of nostalgic flair and a commitment to timeless recipes.

→Augartenbrücke, 1020
→0660 3602277

T O U C H

Mühlbauer Hutmanufaktur

Counting Yoko Ono and Madonna among their past patrons, Mühlbauer provides a shopping experience of both high quality and diversity. All fabrics and styles are assembled and brought to you according to the season of your choice. Their hats are unique and they manage to mix tradition with a modern touch.

→Seilergasse 10, 1010
→01 5122241

Büro Weltausstellung

A young, free-form exhibition space of the Vienna Art Foundation. The focus is on contemporary art, many times with a touch of socio-political critique.

→Praterstraße 42, 1020

Scheer Massschuhe

Since 1816, the Scheer family has crafted bespoke shoes by hand in Vienna, blending seven generations of knowledge and craftsmanship, and producing fewer than 300 pairs annually from its historic location. Esteemed worldwide and bearing a rich Austrian tradition as former purveyors to the Imperial and Royal Court.

→Bräunerstraße 4, 1010
→01 5329892

Kutschkermarkt

The Kutschkermarkt, located in Vienna's 18th district, hosts a weekly farmer's market alongside its permanent stalls, offering a range of products including fruit, vegetables, bread, and cheese. Visitors can find a variety of eateries and specialty food stalls, such as Mayr Delikatessen for cheese and Takan's Delikatessen for seafood. Additionally, various cafes and small restaurants around the market, like Café Himmelblau and Cafébrennerei Franze, offer places to dine and enjoy coffee.

→Kutschkermarkt, 1180

S M E L L

Pratersauna

One of Vienna's infamous nightclubs is set in a former public lido and sauna house. A good plan for any season, it's especially great for hot summer nights thanks to an outdoor pool area. Come to rub elbows with the city's young underground techno-heads.

→Waldsteingartenstraße 135, 1020

Loos American Bar

"Don't be afraid of being criticized for being unfashionable. Changes to the old construction are only permitted if they mean an improvement but otherwise stick with the old one. Because the truth, even if it is hundreds of years old, has more connection with us than the lie that walks alongside us.- Adolf Loos, Architect 1870-1933"

→Kärntner Durchgang 10, 1010
→01 5123283

Grelle Forelle

This house and techno nightclub is a good social equaliser—here the posh dance among the alternative and there are no VIPs. It's not Berghain, but its popularity among the locals will mean a lineup at the door and a tricky door policy.

→Spittelauer Lände 12, 1090

H E A R

F I L M

Hundstage, Ulrich Seidl, 2001

This Austrian drama delves into the private lives of several characters during the hottest days of summer. Told in a series of vignettes, the film presents a provocative, uncompromising look at the darker side of suburban life.

ZURICH

“The rattling of the relays of the Z4 was the only interesting thing to be experienced in Zurich’s night-life.”

Konrad Zuse

S E E

Helmhaus

This museum supports Switzerland's contemporary art scene, with a tight focus on artists who live or have lived in Zurich. Every year they install five shows that represent over 100 artists. In summer they show works that were used in applications for grants or residencies overseas, which bridges the Swiss scene's relationship with international audiences.

→Limmatquai 31, 8001
→044 415 56 77

Museum für Gestaltung

Get deep into what Zurich offers in terms of industrial design, visual communication, architecture and craft. The museum's main collection is of international importance,

and the temporary exhibitions are either loaned from big international galleries or incredibly well-curated with a focus on innovation and contemporary trends.

→Pfingstweidstrasse 96, 8005
→043 446 67 67

Museum Haus Konstruktiv

On the outside, the museum serves as an iconic demonstration of industrial architecture. Inside, it is dedicated to contemporary art – particularly concrete, constructive and conceptual. Temporary exhibits come from names such as Max Bill and James Turrell, and the permanent collection is just as impressive.

→Selnaustrasse 25, 8001
→044 217 70 80

Unterer Letten

Unterer Letten, a riverside bathing facility in Zurich, was established in 1909 and is known for its historical significance and original architecture by Fissler and Friedrich. The bathing facility features a swimming channel that allows bathers to drift downstream, a few fight against the current, but most climb ashore and run back.

→Wasserwerkstrasse 141, 8037
→044 413 58 90

Seebad Enge

Zurich in the summer – it's a bliss. The locals call the pools by the lake "Baedis". At Seebad Enge the crowd is young and flirty.

→Mythenquai 9, 8002
→044 201 38 89

T A S T E

Neumarkt

Situated in Zürich's old town, the establishment seeks to be a local inn for visitors, offering straightforward dishes and supplementing traditional Zürich cuisine with vegetarian specialties. It boasts a garden restaurant in its courtyard and also operates Bauernschänke and Neue Taverne, maintaining traditions and focusing on producers from the Zürich region across its Bistro, Café Bar, and garden restaurant.

→Neumarkt, 8001

Kronenhalle

This restaurant has been a local favourite since the 1920s, so they must be doing something right. It could be the high-quality gourmet regional cuisine, the fine cocktails, the historical art lining the romantic wood-panelled walls, the proud service or the hearty "Zürcher Geschnetzeltes with Rösti". Perhaps all of the above.

→Rämistrasse 4, 8001
→044 262 99 00

Josef

When you're done with the city's slick restaurants and traditional cuisine, tap into the creativity at this restaurant. Preferably on a Friday or Saturday when they have DJs playing. The food, with a creative Mediterranean influence, is fantastic and the interior is so playfully decorated. The menu isn't divided into starters and mains, it's more about ordering small plates until you aren't hungry anymore.

→Gasometerstrasse 24, 8005
→044 271 65 95

Rosso

Industrial without so much chic—Rosso is hidden in a converted warehouse with no sign outside to direct you in. Book or face a fair wait for a place at the shared tables—and then bask in pizza paradise. From the paper-thin crust to the sauce, the pies are made from scratch and with love. They're served by staff adept at navigating the large, rowdy groups of diners that fill the huge space up after dusk. Lunchtime is a slightly quieter affair

→Geroldstrasse 31, 8005
→043 818 22 54

Cafe Noir

Every city has an assortment of places claiming "the best coffee in town"—but the blend at Café Noir is served up in bars all over Zurich, so there might be something to it. Since opening in 2006 with an authentic 1960s coffee roaster and a Dalla Corte espresso machine, it's become a star in the city's coffeescape. Varieties are available separately as well as blended, and sold to take away—whole, hand- or electric-ground. Parts for various coffee machines are stocked, showing they mean business. And the tiny, stylish interior is perfect for observing the particular crowd coming through.

→Neugasse 33, 8005
→044 558 34 10

Eisenhof

It might look like an old-school diner in a train station, but Eisenhof is a legendary stop owing to another retro form of transport. Namely, horse. A juicy 250g filet of horsemeat is the specialty at this unpretentious joint bang in the middle of Zurich's trend zone. Though beef and cordon bleu are also offered, the sheer tastiness of the equine option is guaranteed to dissolve all moral scruples. Served rare on hot stones—so you can continue to cook it as you please—the steak draws in a crowd of faithful old-timers along with an increasing percentage of youngsters too.

→Gasometerstrasse 20, 8005
→044 271 39 90

Wirtschaft Degenried

Venture into the forest for a hearty meal at this restaurant. The interior is super cosy, the menu classic, and the prices reasonable. The surroundings, though, are grand.

→Degenriedstrasse 135, 8032
→044 381 51 80

Bauernschänke

After years of honing his skills in the luxury gastronomy sector, chef Nenad Mlinarevic decided to go back to basics and opened his own restaurant in Zurich's Old Town, inside what used to be the historic Bauenschänke. He kept the name but updated the interior as well as the menu, which features strictly local ingredients that are creatively combined. A lot of people come for the roasted pork belly as well as the homemade bread and lemonade.

→Rindermarkt 24, 8001
→044 262 41 30

Zum Goldenen Fass

The young owners of this restaurant have created a humble and homely vibe in the city's red light district. The menu is a fresh and soulful collision of Swiss and Mediterranean flavours inspired by mami and nonna. Get the baked whole trout or braised pork belly, followed by the sorbet with vodka or fresh figs with grappa.

→Europaallee 17, 8004
→044 260 44 44

T O U C H

Uhren Atelier

The tiny vintage watch shop is seemingly an old-school kiosk whose main responsibility is to distribute gum among passersby, the atelier is actually filled with hundreds of restored timepieces. Don't be put off by the cheaper models in the window– earn the maestro's trust and he'll unveil his sleek Daytonas and classy Pateks.

→Rindermarkt 21, 8001
→044 262 60 90

VMC

This store is all about blue jeans, with neat piles of everything from 501s to 11MWs stacked high to the ceiling. But the heritage store is no one trick pony—there's plenty on offer including vintage shirts, outerwear and a grand selection of leather boots.

→Rindermarkt 8, 8001
→044 251 56 96

enSoie

Monique Meier started enSoie in 1974 by buying Zurich silk producer Brauchbar & Sons. She started off producing silk scarves with prints designed by famous Swiss artists. These days the whole Meier clan works for enSoie in one capacity or another. They say that they produce "for the soul, not for sale" which perfectly sums up their socially conscious approach to all their products from their clothes to the accessories and handcrafted ceramics

→Strehlgasse 26, 8001
→044 211 59 02

Max Chocolatier

Max Chocolatier Shop is a delight for chocolate enthusiasts, crafting unique and seasonally inspired chocolate creations using premium, natural ingredients. From Marc de Champagne chocolates in winter, Passionfruit "Schoggi Plättli" in summer

→Schlüsselgasse 12, 8001
→044 251 03 33

Confiserie Teuscher

"Confiserie Teuscher is a real Zurich original. And even though the confectionery now has branches all over the world, the classic champagne truffles and chocolate pralines are best had in the main store on Storchengasse.

→Bahnhofstrasse 46, 8001
→044 211 13 90

SMELL

Züri Bar

Since the 1950s, the Züri Bar in the heart of Zurich's old town has been a meeting place for students, musicians, journalists and neighbourhood residents. It now focuses on Italian aperitifs and antipasti.

→Niederdorfstrasse 24, 8001
→076 250 37 41

Panama

This summer-only, riverside terrace may not look like much but makes for a perfect place to unwind on a hot Zurich day, possibly after a dip in the Oberen Letten. The bar/grill offers numerous food and drink options, including a weekend brunch. Beware though, it can get busy in peak season, so expect lines.

→Lettensteg 10, 8037

Ole Ole Bar

Pouring drinks to locals for over 50 years, this bar has watched the hood go from seedy to seedier to eventually winding up–as these areas tend to do–as Zurich's night spot. Pop in and mix with the locals, and maybe even get some tips on where to head next.

→Langstrasse 138, 8004
→044 242 91 39

Gonzo

Dive bar meets club - another stop to have a few drinks on Zurich's bar mile Langstrasse. You might not spot the entrance, but follow the queue–it leads to the graffitied basement, a small dance floor and more "mexikaner" shots than you can handle.

→Langstrasse 135, 8004

Rio Bar

More a flexible daytime place than a bar. Located right on the little river Sihl this is an unpretentious hang-out for everything from breakfast to after-work beer. In summer the terrace is perfect for observing the passersby, listening to the river wash by, and enjoying some dolce far niente in the sun.

→Gessnerallee 17, 8001
→043 244 09 09

H E A R

F I L M

Die Schweizermacher, Rolf Lyssy, 1978

This satirical Swiss film explores the lives of two men tasked with the duty of assessing citizenship applicants. Through a mix of humour and drama, it paints an insightful picture of Swiss society and its views on immigration during the late 70s.

Publishing Details
LOST iN, Issue No.25, Europe

Editorial Office: Lost in the City GmbH

Editor-in-Chief: Uwe Hasenfuss (ViSdP)

Managing Director: Joseph Djenandji

Art Direction & Design: NODE Berlin Oslo
(Serge Rompza, Georg Stahlbock)
node.international

Photography: Iwan Baan, Johanna Berstein, Diego Delso,
Austin Feilders, Roland Fischer, Bernard Gagnon,
Lukas Gansterer, Jörg Henning, Heinrich Klaffs,
Sebastian Koppehel, Kristo, Marsan, Miguel Martinez,
Olaf Meister, Sharon Molerus, Patrick Mueller,
Jonathan Niclaus, Natalia Recchia, Serge Rompza,
Hubert Saint Olive, Rainer Serrat, Rudolph Simon,
Kim Traynor, Robert Valette, Marco Verch,
Manfred Werner, Felix Wong

Printing: ORT Medienverbund GmbH, Germany

ISBN 978-3-946647-25-6

Inquiries: info@lostin.com
lostin.com

Fore Cover:
Bruno Munari, Faces, 1966

Rear Cover:
The Miriam and Ira D. Wallach Division of Art, Prints
and Photographs: Picture Collection, The New York
Public Library. “Europa on the back of Zeus in the form
of a bull” The New York Public Library Digital
Collections. 1872–1887.